T0345478

Festivals in Focus

Festivals in Focus
Dragan Klaic

With an Introduction by
Christopher Maughan
and Franco Bianchini

Including The Future of
European Festivals by
Bernard Faivre d'Arcier

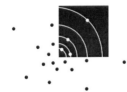

THE BUDAPEST OBSERVATORY

Budapest, Hungary

Published in 2014 by

Regional Observatory on Financing Culture in East-Central Europe
(The Budapest Observatory)
Október 6. utca 14, H-1051 Budapest, Hungary
Tel: +36-1-327-3829
Fax: +36-1-374-0898
E-mail: bo@budobs.org
Website: www.budobs.org

Distributed by

Central European University Press
Budapest - New York
Nádor utca 11, H-1051 Budapest, Hungary
Tel: +36-1-327-3138
Fax: +36-1-3273183
E-mail: ceupress@ceu.hu
Website: www.ceupress.com

224 West 57th Street, New York NY 10019, USA
Telephone: +1-212-547-6932, Fax: +1-646-557-2416
E-mail: martin.greenwald@opensocietyfoundations.org

ISBN 978-963-08-7940-8

A catalog record for this book is available from the
Library of Congress.

Cover design and layout by Júlia Hentz
Printed in Hungary by Prime Rate Kft.,
CEO: Péter Tomcsányi, PhD.

Contents

Acknowledgements

Special thanks are due to Christopher Maughan and Franco Bianchini for the editorial work undertaken for this book, to Katarina Pejović, Anne-Marie Autissier, Richard Fletcher and Jennie Jordan for their help, and Tom Faber for his translation from the French of the essay by Bernard Faivre d'Arcier.

We would also like to acknowledge the financial support received from the European Cultural Foundation for the production of this book.

Introduction

Christopher Maughan and Franco Bianchini

Whilst Dragan Klaic was principally known as a theatre and cultural policy scholar his interest in festivals was long standing. The Belgrade *International Theatre Festival (Bitef)*, which had been founded in 1967, clearly had a big influence upon him. As Michael Coveney writes in his obituary of Dragan: *"Bitef* became a crucible for the kind of cultural exchanges that Klaic relished ..... a bridge between the explosion in western counterculture and the reconsideration of Slavic and Russian classical traditions."[1]

From 1978-1991 Dragan was Professor of Theatre History and Drama at the University of Arts in

[1] Coveney, M. Klaic, obituary: Theatre scholar and cultural commentator, Guardian, 27 September 2011.

Belgrade and worked as theatre critic for the Belgrade newspaper, *Politika*, from 1982-1984. After the outbreak of the Yugoslav wars in 1991 he left Belgrade and settled in Amsterdam, where he took up the post of Director of Theater Instituut Nederland (TIN) from 1992-2001.

Dragan was prodigiously active in the European cultural management and policy scene, especially from the early 1990s. He contributed to courses organised by many institutions including the universities of Amsterdam, Leiden and Bologna, the Central European University, Budapest and the Fondation Marcel Hicter. He co-founded the European Theatre Quarterly *Euromaske*, and served as the President of the European Forum for the Arts and Heritage (2002-2004). He also acted as the Moderator of the Reflection Group of the European Cultural Foundation (2002-2004) and wrote its final report *Europe as a Cultural Project*[2].

As Anne-Marie Autissier observed at the European Festival Research Project workshop held in Maribor in October 2011:
"Dragan's work focused on building a shared cultural base for Europe, because he felt that the construction of such a base had been neglected."

[2] Klaic, D. et al. Europe as a Cultural Project, Amsterdam: European Cultural Foundation, 2005.

Dragan's awareness of the fact that arts festivals in Europe were an under-researched topic, as well as his recognition of the potential of festivals for developing intercultural competences and a European internationalist consciousness, led him to launch EFRP, the European Festival Research Project.

Dragan's internationalism and curiosity are reflected by the fact that he could communicate in as many as nine languages. His linguistic abilities and his continuous travelling gave him a special knowledge of the continent from the inside, and nurtured his commitment to European values now under threat, such as sustained levels of public spending on culture, education and research, and respect for human rights.

Dragan drew upon this experience and his extensive network of contacts to mobilise researchers and practitioners in support of his vision for EFRP as a network in which important issues concerning artistic festivals could be discussed. Dragan also gave the whole project its intellectual coherence. It was principally through him that the partnerships, the funding and other forms of support required to deliver a regular programme of workshops across Europe were achieved. Evidence of his knowledge of the sector was that many of EFRP's research workshops were delivered in association with an artistic festival. Dragan further supported the network through his charming but sharp chairing and summarising of the workshops.

Despite having no secure financial support except for some funding for its establishment in 2004, the EFRP network managed to operate from 2004-2011. Participants saw it as an opportunity to share research, to create a platform for the presentation of work in progress, for young scholars and practitioners to meet and share their perspectives, and for all to contribute to a new area of knowledge and enquiry, 'festival studies'.

One of Dragan's legacies was the production of four essays with which he intended to introduce the collective volume of the EFRP studies and its various parts respectively. Because of his untimely death these chapters have to be seen in part as work in progress. Nonetheless, these four essays display his sharp critical ability and raise many interesting questions about festivals not just in Europe but in a global context.

Of Dragan's four essays the first is the most fully developed, and provides a sense of the historical, religious, social and cultural underpinning required to understand and discuss more contemporary developments in artistic festivals.

In his second essay Dragan provides an analysis of different types of festivals. This extends his focus on the artistic and international qualities that he associated with artistic festivals and which he argued could enable them to make a special contribution to the development of 'Europe as a cultural project', something that Krzysztof Czyżewski and Anne-Marie Autissier write about in their personal tributes. A frequent observation that Dragan made of much festivals research was that it was driven by criteria and perspectives that had more to do with the instrumental function and (social, economic, educational, image) impacts of festivals than with their artistic goals and content. He was constant in his encouragement of all researchers to expand their horizons and to work outside of their own local, regional and national contexts to explore international perspectives and comparisons across and between countries.

Dragan's third essay explores programming policies and practices as another critical feature of the distinction that he makes between artistic and other festivals. Dragan identifies a range of different strategies but at the heart of his discussion is the explicit requirement that the programme should represent a well researched and coherent engagement with the artistic product. His argument about the need for a significant travel budget is one that many artistic directors will appreciate, especially when funding for the arts is under pressure. Dragan links to this discussion the capacity of festivals to integrate education activities into their programmes, either in the close season or during the festival itself. In this and other aspects of his discussion the relationship between festival organisations and funding partners is examined. The latter can often have a significant impact on a festival's programme, where the event seeks to justify public or private sector investment through opportunist programming of elements of activity that are priorities for the funder.

In his final essay Dragan draws attention to the relationship between a festival and the space or place where it is delivered. Urban festivals, rural festivals, festivals located in unusual sites are all considered in his overview of how space and place can influence artistic programming and how audiences contribute to this through a change in their engagement with the locality. Dragan again emphasises the importance of developing international perspectives on this in terms of choice of programme and how to use space/place as part of a successful festival programme.

The book is concluded with an essay by Bernard Faivre d'Arcier, who was twice director of the *Avignon Festival*. Whilst providing a personal reflection, Faivre d'Arcier echoes many of

Dragan's own thoughts and analysis in particular his concern that festivals must be driven by a focus on artistic creativity and operate as a place where artists can dare to take risks.

Two themes are at the heart of this book. The first is the insight to be gained about the role festivals can and do play in contemporary life. This includes the need to understand the social, cultural, political, economic and physical context in which festivals are operating. This in turn should prompt us to think about the 'festivalisation' of everyday life as a mobilising process in terms of how audiences come to engage with and enjoy the arts. But we should also reflect on how artistic festivals can make a deeper contribution when they seek to connect with other cultural traditions, especially if they are international in their reach and ambitions.

The second insight is to the understanding that Dragan Klaic himself had of the fragile world of festivals. Dragan thought that festivals, predominantly artistic festivals with an international agenda and publicly funded, could play a significant role in the delivery of a more international approach to arts programming, to audience development, and integration with local policy agendas ranging from economic development and tourism to education and social policy. Finally we see in his advocacy and promotion of EFRP, in his encouragement of a more longitudinal and collegiate approach to research and his expectation of critical reflection how profoundly he believed that festivals had the potential (denied to many continuously operating organisations which may be locked into funding agreements with an expectation of specific outcomes) to explore a more risk-oriented arts agenda. An agenda which brought them close to a key feature of his life's work: the idea of 'Europe as a cultural project'.

© Tory Rodrigue

"Dragan Klaic's faith in festivals as a uniting cultural force seems to have had much in common with the altruistic beginnings of the *Edinburgh Festival*. While it is true that post-war Edinburgh desperately needed new economic drivers, there is no reason to doubt the founders' desires for a cultural framework that might help to pull Europe together again. Dragan's desire was to deconstruct the silos of national identity, and construct in their place platforms on which the differences in language and practice could be better understood and shared. While Melina Mercouri's desires for better understanding between the different cultures of Europe resulted in many positive collaborations and much-needed sources of mobility for artists through the European Capital of Culture programme, the programme has also bred a kind of necessary civic bragging that I doubt Dragan would have found productive."

Robyn Archer, Creative Director of the Centenary of *Canberra*, former Artistic Director of *Adelaide* and *Melbourne Festival*

Festivals is Focus

Dragan Klaic

A Historical Perspective

The origins of today's festivals can be traced back to ancient feasts and celebrations of a ritual character, as societies and social groups sought to punctuate the flow of ordinary time with special occasions and endow them with meaning as symbolic affirmations of a community's continuity and welfare. Whether they expressed allegiance to supernatural powers, their ancestors or current rulers, societies created a sequence of ritualised actions and deeds that symbolically reinforced their hierarchies, sense of the self and value systems. These festivals occurred at fixed times in the course of the year, marked by the changes of the seasons, and realigned society with nature.

Celebratory activities, albeit inspired by religious beliefs, sometimes implied some pragmatic considerations, as well. Festivals in Ancient Greece celebrating the god Dionysus in the 5th century BC at the same time helped entrench symbolically the dominance of Athens over other city states, by soliciting their gifts to the Dionysius temple in Athens. Roman festivities, especially in the imperial period, stressed entertainment over strictly religious functions and served to appease the masses and secure their allegiance to the rulers or power contenders.

In the Christian calendar, Biblical narratives and especially the New Testament rendering of Jesus' life marked the festive moments of the year, additionally filled later with the special days of celebration of the Virgin Mary and of the saints. Medieval mystery plays, performed across Europe in a stunning variety of forms and logistic arrangements, tended to mark the Corpus Christi holiday and asserted festive performance over all other activities of urban life, expanding gradually from the interior of the church to the city streets and squares, especially in the processional model practiced in England. These large participative festivals depended on the contribution of many volunteers in the preparatory works and in the performance itself, and served to assert the value, richness and skills of a city over other neighbouring places, thus nurturing local pride.

Similarly, medieval fairs were exceptional, rather dense gatherings of sellers and buyers but also rare opportunities for enjoyment, pleasure and intensive socializing, enhanced by some performances that stressed the festive character of the event above its commercial function.

Renaissance and later baroque court festivals catered to a more elite audience of aristocrats and courtiers, and sought to praise the ruler, often through intricate analogies with mythological characters, to express the loyalty of his subjects to him. Whether young aristocrats, students or servants appeared in these feasts as performers, they were celebrants and were specifically assigned characters within an elaborate narrative of great symbolic aspiration, which followed a complex staging plan, seeking to evoke pleasure and admiration. Festive procession, triumphal entries into the city, celebration of peace and of aristocratic weddings and births completed the repertory of such proto-festivals, multiplying the formulae and technical and logistical arrangements with special skills and machinery to create stunning effects and of course to spend considerable budgets.

An early blueprint of today's festival practice can be found in the plan of English actor David Garrick to celebrate the anniversary of Shakespeare's birth by staging in September 1769 a festive procession of actors, dressed as Shakespeare's characters in the bard's birthplace, Stratford upon Avon. Confirming the 18th century status of Shakespeare as a cultural hero, so many visitors descended on the small town in Midlands of England that, unprepared for so much attention, Stratford quickly ran out of food, beer and ale whilst the English weather predictably spoiled the procession. Garrick lost a lot of his own money in this festive operation and later mocked his own ambition in the self-ironic one-act play *The Jubilee*. This incident is an early lesson to all subsequent festival managers about the inherent risk, logistical complexity and dependence on weather conditions that can wreck even the best festival concept.

The French Revolution sought to eliminate the influence of the Catholic Church and abolished the Christian calendar replacing it with its own revolutionary scheme of time, with decades instead of weeks and new names for the months, starting the count from the first year of the revolution and the attack by the masses on the Bastille. The revolution also sought to mobilize the masses and secure their loyalty through symbolic representation of their purpose and mission, celebrating Reason as the Supreme Being instead of the pantheon of Christian saints. Such revolutionary festivities could also be seen within the proto-festival evolution of celebratory forms, with processions, enactments, the deployment of artistic talent and the promotion of revolutionary symbols, with the aim of making the erratic political project of the revolution appear as predetermined and inevitable. And yet, the key festival act of the French Revolution was the literal elimination of its proclaimed enemies through the mass spectacle of the guillotine at work. Once the revolution speeded up the production of enemies and made their elimination a daily occurrence in the months of mass terror, the festive character was lost and replaced by the turgid display of the senseless killing machinery.

During the 19th century, festivals gradually took shape as festive clusters of concerts, especially in the German tradition of *Festspiele*, switching gradually from aristocratic patronage to the service of an enlightened bourgeoisie and its needs for status elevation and self-respect, especially through solemn dedication to artistic music, sacred and secular. This musical orientation of festivals was complemented by other, more popular forms of feasts, combining the demonstration of skills, sport, traditional art forms, eating and drinking and some intensive trade to profit from the assembled crowd of potential customers. Artistic, cultural, social and economic aspects were intertwined and reinforced each other, and the places where such *Festspiele* took place expected to benefit materially and symbolically, to boost the local economy and prestige, while being nominally interested only in the advancement of the arts.

Richard Wagner's festive season in Bayreuth which began in 1876 was also driven by a complex agenda: to affirm his notion of music drama as a solemn cultural exercise that reinforced the nation in its identity and sense of historic purpose, against the trivial tradition of opera and its performance as court entertainment, catering to aristocratic vanity, or as a bourgeois leisure time option. At the same time, the production and performances of his opus in a concentrated time span in Bayreuth enabled Wagner to affirm himself as the foremost artist of the nation and its spiritual guide. The considerable appeal of Wagner's densely packed festive programme exercised a substantial appeal for German and foreign music lovers and elites, merging artistic and social, even socialite interests. However, even this recipe could not make the *Festspiele* economically sustainable; having almost bankrupted its producer and key artist, it had to be rescued by the generous contribution of Wagner's mentor, King Ludwig II.

Looking at the antecedents of today's festival practice, one can briefly note the stagings by

8

the French actor Firmin Gémier[3] together with amateurs from the Swiss side of Lake Geneva, meant as some modern-day invocation of winegrowers' and fishermen traditions and lore but most probably a barely disguised tourism boosting stratagem, dressed up in bucolic clothes. The event that more closely models a contemporary festival matrix is the Salzburg *Festpiele* as created and led by Max Reinhardt after World War One. Defeated and dismembered, weakened politically and exhausted economically, with the bitter nostalgic mythology of a lost empire as its key symbolic capital, Austria could seek to regain status among other European countries only through culture. The baroque architecture of Salzburg offered a spectacular setting for Reinhardt's ambition to recreate theatre as a major neo-baroque event that fascinated and captivated a large public, erased the barriers of class and education and transcended the increased commercialization of art as entertainment and commodity. Aided by the poetic and dramatic talent of Hugo von Hofmannsthal, Reinhardt recreated theatre as a dominant event of urban life, staging *Jedermann* in front of the Salzburg cathedral, as a replica of the medieval mysteries and moralities.

[3] Firmin Gémier (1869-1933), French actor and theatre director.

Jedermann was in fact a contemporary rendering of the 15th century Flemish-English morality play, *Elckerlijc-Everyman*, which connected the medieval notions of *ars moriendi*, the pious Christian preparation for death, to bourgeois anxieties about material affluence, made worthless by the inevitability and unpredictability of death. In the Hofmannsthal-Reinhardt version, death appears as a democratic, even egalitarian crushing force, a final leveller of socio-economic distinctions, otherwise carefully nurtured by a bourgeois morality which relativised the moral problems raised by wealth accumulation, and affirmed the sanctity of private property and the tacit assumptions of privilege and exemption that money can buy. This *Jedermann*, made in 1920 for the world of certainties crushed by the World War One and the ensuing revolutions, was further supplemented by other Reinhardt stagings in convenient and appealing Salzburg sites, inside sumptuous palaces and convent courtyards, making him a pioneer of today's performative appropriation and recycling of space, of site specific theatre and festival buzz and éclat. With Reinhardt as its undisputed artistic leader and magician-in-residence, encircled by famous conductors, singers and musicians, the Salzburg *Festpiele* became a gathering point of cultural elites and high society, an artistic and cosmopolitan stronghold against Austrian cultural traditionalism and provincialism – at least until 1938 when Hitler's *Anschluss* made Reinhardt and so many of his colleagues, collaborators and guests seek refuge in exile.

The history of contemporary festivals continued to unfold only after the ravages of World War Two, when the festival formulae needed to be reinvented and advanced in order to assert the values of culture against hatred, brutality and persecution. Festivals became celebrations of humanity, its talent and creativity and collaborative will, an investment in the virtues of citizenship in post-war democracies, an inspiring and encouraging force that reasserted a promise of future peace, stability and prosperity in Europe, despite the tensions and anxieties caused by the escalating Cold War. While the Salzburg *Festspiele* was relaunched in 1945, two post-war festivals emerged in 1947 in two very different places. The first was the Scottish capital of Edinburgh, which met the criteria outlined by Sir Rudolf Bing[4] for a location that could accommodate large numbers of visitors in a place of great scenic beauty and be committed to a festival that could "provide a platform for the flowering of the human

[4] Sir Rudolf Bing (1902-1917), one of the founders of the Edinburgh International Festival and its first Director from1947-49; also General Manager of Glyndebourne Opera Festival from 1935-45.

spirit". The second, as a result of the initiative of actor Jean Vilar[5], was Avignon, a sleepy historic town of Provence in Southern France, with splendid and monumental medieval palaces of popes.

Edinburgh reflected a democratisation of culture perspective on the role and value of the arts as embodied also in the founding aims of the Arts Council of Great Britain in 1946.

Avignon inspired Vilar as a place where an audience of some 3,000 could be presented with emblematic works of the dramatic tradition, and experience the magic of arts as a new civic religion, much before mass tourism, jet travel and the TGV. Soon after the launch of the Avignon summer programme Vilar was given an opportunity to test his strategy for the democratization of culture by directing productions of French dramatic classics for the enormous auditorium of Palais de Chaillot in Paris, which was filled to a great extent by beneficiaries of reduced group ticket schemes, distributed through trade union channels.

While Edinburgh sought a balance among music, drama and ballet and relied much on invited artists, British and foreign, Vilar as a proud patron

[5] Jean Vilar (1912-1971), French actor and theatre director.

of Palais de Chaillot kept Avignon jealously as his summer base and the entire programme of the several early editions of the festival was filled by his company and his productions only.

From this point on the festival sector in Europe experienced rapid change. In 1948 the *Holland Festival* started in Amsterdam, The Hague, Rotterdam and Utrecht, again driven by ideas of democratization of culture and by the ambition to compensate with prominent foreign artists for the rather provincial circumstances of the post-war Dutch cultural scene. In the early 1950s photographs by Kors van Bennekom one can see the long line of people encircling the Amsterdam Municipal theatre, waiting patiently for long hours to buy *Holland Festival* tickets as the entry into a precious world of artistic adventure and excitement. Van Bennekom's pictures offer a convincing demonstration of the public's hunger for a special cultural offer that might make today's *Holland Festival* marketers envious.

In 1950, Dubrovnik, another walled city of well preserved medieval and Renaissance architecture, launched the *Dubrovnik Summer Festival*, with productions of Greek tragedies, Shakespeare's plays and Dubrovnik Renaissance authors, staged on the city's ramparts and fortresses, with classic music concerts and poetry recitals in the courtyards and patios of convents and palaces, on the beaches and in parks. Tito had two years before broken with Stalin and sought to legitimise his rule as an alternative type of socialism, so a summer festival on the Croatian Adriatic coast was a convenient project through which to present/promote a new, more liberal cultural policy, secure the loyalty of the domestic intelligentsia and send some encouraging signals abroad. The programme gave prominence to both domestic and world classics and revived them in the fascinating ambiance of a dense urban space. There was hardly any tourism, domestic or foreign, in Yugoslavia at the time. The county was mobilising all its scarce resources to fight Soviet pressure and military menace and survived thanks to shyly accepted Western aid, but the festival in Dubrovnik was a prestige project set up by the Government to prove that it was moving away from Soviet-style drabness and ideological narrow-mindedness. In a short time the Dubrovnik Summer festival became a precious window to the world and a privileged stage on which many Western artists first appeared in Yugoslavia.

During this period it is important to remember the impact of the grip of the Cold War confrontation on culture. Culturally as well as ideologically, Europe was divided by the Iron Curtain but classical music festivals began to proliferate under the assumption that this artistic idiom escaped ideological appropriations and manipulations, that music represented the shared cultural treasury of humanity and that in music only talent counts, not political associations and interests. Of course, that is a rather naïve and quite elitist assumption, and today we know that the Boston Symphony Orchestra's European tours in 1952 and 1956 had been arranged by the CIA via the Paris-based Congress for Cultural Freedom and funded by CIA through some bogus private foundations, in order to attempt counter the appeal of Soviet culture to the European leftist intelligentsia. Moreover, Europe's first festival of contemporary music was arranged in Rome by the CIA operative Nikolas Nabokov[6].

In Switzerland, philosopher Denis de Rougemont[7] strove to sustain the unity of European culture despite ideological and political rifts. In his view - and he had plausible anti-communist credentials – culture has a role as a bridge across growing political differences. In a 1951 article, written with the conductor Igor Markevitch, he noted the fast emergence of classical music festivals

[6] Nikolas (Nikolai) Nabokov (1903-1978), Russian-born composer, writer, and cultural figure.
[7] Denis de Rougemont (1906-1985), Swiss writer, cultural theorist, and European federalist.

and by 1952 he had established the European Association of Music Festivals, one of many of his European cultural initiatives. There were hardly a dozen regularly occurring music festivals at the time in Europe. De Rougemont was a visionary who helped define the festival template and who plunged into festival politics with an understanding that this emerging type of artistic celebration had the potential to re-assert the unity of European cultural space and enhance artistic mobility within its confines.

UNESCO, established in 1945 as part of the UN institutional system of intergovermental politics, initiated a range of international organisations for various artistic domains. The International Theatre Institute, based in UNESCO's Paris headquarters, convened regular congresses where representatives of national ITI committees could meet, talk to each other and debate the perspectives of the performing arts in the world, and thus use professional discourse as a shield against Cold War animosities. In order to give some visibility to its activities and demonstrate the artistic potential of its worldwide constituency ITI launched the *World Theatre Season* in Paris as a *de facto* festival in 1954. The appearance of Brecht's Berliner Ensemble from East Berlin broke the political blockade of the GDR in the West and created a lasting impression on the French and international theatre profession, seeding numerous Brechtians and Brechtologists and proving in a way that world theatre indeed means unexpected confrontations but also the spreading of aesthetic influences and affinities across borders. In a world that had reluctantly just entered the turbulent decolonisation process all the ambitions of showing the world theatre in a single festival inevitably remained more a matter of rhetoric than of a plausible deed. After several years the ITI initiative lost the necessary support, only to be revived in Paris much later, in 1972, as a French governmental project, launched by Michel Guy[8] and known as *Festival d'automne à Paris*, more a stretched festive season of international appearances than a condensed festival programme. The same cosmopolitan and holistic ambition to represent the world of theatre as ITI attempted in the 1950s drove Sir Peter Daubeny[9] in the 1960s to develop his *World Theatre Season* in London as an alternative to the self-centredness of English theatre at the time and to the West End's addiction to transfers from Broadway.

Music festivals and theatre festivals proliferated in the 1950s and the European festival tableau was further filled with the growing popularity

[8] Michel Guy (1927-1990), French cultural figure and politician.
[9] Sir Peter Daubeny (1921- 1975), German-born British theatre impresario.

17

of film festivals. Feature films festivals were driven by the market opportunities they enhanced. *Cannes Film Festival*, originally planned for 1940 and cancelled because of the outbreak of the war, finally got established in 1946, followed by other similar festivals. In the democratic Italian Republic, the *Venice Film Festival* came back into respectability in 1954, having rid itself of the fascist shadow that had followed it since its foundation in 1932. Even in the field of short and documentary film, for instance, *Westdeutsche Kulturfilmtage*, launched in Oberhausen in 1954, grew into a prominent international festival of this chiefly non-commercial aspect of film art.

In the focal point of the Cold War, in West Berlin, where the continuity of Western cultural presence was perceived at the time as a strategic matter of war and peace, Berliner *Festspiele* (today a mighty cluster of festival initiatives and projects) emerged from its initial programming in 1951 that sought to reduce the West Berliner's sense of isolation and vulnerability and used the arts as a source of encouragement to civil society. In the same year, the Wagner season was re-launched in Bayreuth by the composer's grandsons, despite the heavy enmeshment of the family with the Nazi regime, soon to become again a meeting point for social and cultural elites, and a focus for snobbery, prestige and much aesthetic conservativism, surpassed only once the enterprise was reconstructed and financially consolidated in 1973 as a private-public foundation.

Furthermore, the festival map also became inscribed with amateur festivals, festivals of arts for children, and festivals of popular music. With the advancement of television, initially everywhere in Europe a jealously guarded state monopoly, the *Eurovision Song Contest*, established in 1956 by the European Broadcasting Union, became one of the longest running television shows in the world, with a huge and rapidly raising international audience as television sets became a mandatory part of the living room inventory of affluent and later also less affluent Europeans.

The Council of Europe, charged among other tasks, with the furthering of cultural co-operation, published an ambitious document in 1954, the European Cultural Convention, which while it did not mention festivals explicitly, encouraged festival practice. By contrast, the European Economic Community (later the European Union) was a latecomer to encouraging cultural activities, having concentrated on the build up of a common market through economic and employment policy. It addressed film, radio and television as parts of the cultural industry and media market long before it turned to culture as live arts and cultural heritage.

What characterised most of the artistic festivals that emerged in the first 15-20 years after the end of the World War Two was the strong lead/role taken by nation states and the greater availability of governmental financial support, meaning that festivals became part of the emancipatory engagement of the welfare state with its citizens and at the same time a vehicle for many states' representational needs and aspirations. Many festivals were launched with a compensatory purpose behind their programmes, which were expected to enrich with an international dimension what the regular domestic, cultural production sector could not offer throughout the year.

The international dimension was implemented despite the political restrictions emanating from the Cold War context, which oscillated with the shifts in East-West tensions. International programming was affected by budgetary restrictions and by considerable lack of information about current cultural productions across the borders, especially outside the major and traditional cultural centres, and especially behind the Iron Curtain. Both international communication and international travel were constrained by the logistic and technological limitations of the time and consequently some of the festivals articulated their international programming through a request by the organisers, conveyed through diplomatic channels, to the authorities of another country to simply send their own representative piece of art to the festival. Aesthetic considerations, selection, and programming coherence inevitably suffered under such circumstances. International cultural events were by default prestigious and much covered by the media because they were such a rarity.

In the Soviet bloc, where being sent abroad by one's own authorities on a cultural mission was considered a top reward for one's ideological trustworthiness, going to the West was a rare privilege, reserved only for the most loyal and prominent artists, often accompanied by guardians from the political police, who were supposed to ensure proper behaviour and make sure that all the stars came back from the West despite all its temptations. Among the Eastern Bloc countries cultural communication was officially arranged and amply funded, so that all sorts of festivals that emerged in the 1950s and 1960s could count on appearances by artists and artistic work from the 'brotherly' socialist camp, carefully selected by ministry of culture and party ideological officials of the sending country according to their proper representational qualities.

The compensatory and display purpose of established artistic festivals may have been experienced by some participants as an irritant or as a source of frustration, especially when the artistic and political agendas clashed, or when the protocol procedures worked as a snub rather than as enhancement of prestige or flattery, or when the artists felt packaged, used and constrained, reduced to the small wheels of a big political mechanism with its own notions of spectacle and effectiveness. Inevitably, ideas of other, alternative festival formats appeared in the late 1960s, as part of the contesting, anti-authoritarian and anti-paternalistic impulse of younger and not yet established artists. As the great cultural revolution started advancing throughout Europe, driven by US influences and by its own domestic energies and frustrations, artists became less patient and docile and more radical and rebellious. They started twisting or rejecting some of the established festival concepts, formats, conventions of presentation and communication with the pubic and the media. The seed of a new generation of 'alternative', 'off' and 'underground' festivals, as they called themselves, could be seen in the festivals of student theatre, amateur for sure but ambitious and of a strong experimental and critical bent, and soon accomplished or self-assured enough to establish their own international infrastructure that ensured

22

cross border circulation of leading figures and their work. Student theatre festivals in Nancy, Erlangen, Zagreb and Wrocław broke through the Iron Curtain and revealed a surprising degree of shared generational affinities, concerns and idiosyncrasies, despite all their cultural, political and ideological differences.

A new generation of artistic festivals asserted its alternative and oppositional nature in a mixture of artistic disciplines and genres, combining a broad palette of the performing arts species with various sorts of music, film and happenings that in themselves created a histrionic zone between the visual and the performing arts. The political and critical energy of those festivals was fed much by the opposition to the US intervention in Southeast Asia, but expanded to encompass power, hierarchy and control issues closer to home. These festivals asserted an informal lifestyle in celebration of freedom, pleasure and joy. They manifested themselves as radical and often sardonic critics of mainstream politics and established cultural orders. The *Amsterdam Festival of Fools* started in 1975 with a mocking contestation of the *Holland Festival*, itself firmly established in the meantime in the Dutch cultural infrastructure. As its antithesis, the *Festival of Fools* redeployed and extended the symbolic gestures of dissent of tomato throwers from the famous (infamous?)

Aktie Tomaat[10](1969) that brought down the Dutch performing arts system and initiated its restructuring on the basis of many small theatre initiatives and experimental groups, endowed for the first time with government funding.

Since most alternative festivals could not secure access to mainstream cultural venues, they needed to establish their spatial bases by improvisation and temporary appropriation, breaking out of the traditional cultural zones into neglected, marginal or abandoned sites, such as former factories or farms, and chunks of usurped countryside, thus stressing their own alternative character by the very location and the manner of its usage by the festival. The consequences were aesthetic as much as sociological: site-inspired and site-specific performances altered the perception of the urban outskirts, and brought a culturally curious and adventurous public to marginal communities where not much cultural programming normally happened. They induced temporary cohabitation by social groups that did not habitually interact. Such festivals challenged the established

[10] Dutch: Tomato Action. A radical movement in Dutch theater in the late 1960s and early 1970s. It was sparked by an incident in 1969, when students of the Toneelschool (Amsterdam's School of Drama) threw tomatoes at actors performing with the Nederlandse Comedie in Amsterdam's municipal theater.

hierarchies of cultural space, decentralized cultural interventions and made participation in a festival a journey for the audience into the unknown, a discovery, almost an adventure.

Throughout the 1970s and 1980s mainstream artistic festivals sought often to wriggle out of their representational corset and to capture some of the experimental drift and histrionic energy of their new competitors and alternative challengers, by creating special programme series, in parallel to the main programme, and through other tactics of absorption and appeasement, best described by Herbert Marcuse's notion of repressive tolerance. The *Avignon Festival* itself barely survived the scandal the New York Living Theater created there in 1968, with a performance erupting in a tentative march on the local jail to liberate the prisoners and ultimately ending up as a riot. Subsequently, Avignon learned to change and go with the times, to nurture controversy and handle it skilfully, and in 1969 established an international stage for young performing arts professionals. The *Venice Biennale*, with its trio of film, music and theatre festivals, set up a similar stage in 1969 in order to absorb and channel protest, dissent and criticism by young people.

From the mid 1970s Europe saw a steady renewal of its festival scene, the invention of new festival concepts and formulae and increasingly the engagement of local and regional authorities in the funding of festivals. Festivals sought to shake off elitist connotations and to position themselves as democratic, enlightened and open-minded cultural programmes, to unburden themselves of traditionalism and routine. In France, where the socialist Minister of Culture Jack Lang doubled the national cultural budget from 1981 to 1983, an orientation towards large scale cultural events, meant to inspire and engage a large audience, stimulated the proliferation of festivals but also provoked an elitist critique.

The European Festivals Association broadened its mandate to include festivals of other artistic forms than just music and boosted its non-European membership. IETM (Informal European Theatre Meeting) grew rapidly through the 1980s, with a membership encompassing many of the new generation of international festivals, venues with regular international programming, and companies eager to tour internationally and support organisations. Its meetings drew an increased number of participants (over 300 in Bologna in 1988) demanding a certain degree of professionalisation at the expense of informality in order to function as a busy platform of networking, search for partners and co-operation projects.

Since 1985 an expanded European Union, having absorbed the new democracies of Spain, Portugal and Greece, featured the European City of Culture (later renamed European Capital of Culture), a label conferred by the European Commission on one city each year from 1985-1999 (normally two cities from 2001 onwards) which turned it into a site of a year-long mega-festival. After Athens, Florence and Amsterdam, the 1988 European Capital of Culture in West Berlin pointed at the painful realities of the Cold War, felt nowhere as strongly as in the divided city, but also sought to explore potential new channels through the Iron Curtain, made at least conceivable by glasnost and perestroika in the USSR, but then still 'trickling down' with painful slowness to the mindset of the cultural and political apparatchiks of the GDR.

Then, within only a few turbulent months, the compromised communist regimes collapsed all over Central and Eastern Europe. Through the acceptance of multi-party elections, palace coups or popular revolts, the Berlin Wall was broken down, opening the prospect of German reunification, and since 1990 Europe was again imaginable as the integrated cultural space that Denis de Rougemont stubbornly believed in. Festivals rushed to celebrate these new realities and profited in their programming from them, but many were at the same time swept away by the change of political system and the disappearance of their once generous and secure public subsidies. With the disintegration of the USSR and the violent collapse of former Yugoslavia throwing dark shadows on the European cultural stage, a new élan in the construction of Europe inserted a cultural paragraph in the 1992 Treaty of Maastricht, endowing the European Union with limited and conditional cultural competences. Anticipating EU funding of international cultural co-operation, IETM engaged in the advocacy of artistic mobility across Europe, seeking to prompt other cultural networks, cultural producing organisations and especially festivals as expected beneficiaries and key players.

In Central and Eastern Europe systemic cultural changes were less obvious than the changes ushered in by multi-party parliamentary democracy and by the market economy. Most public cultural institutions there continued to operate, more or less disoriented by all the contextual change, shifts in the public attention and curiosity, altered family budgets and much less public money available for culture. Liberated from the humiliating grip of censorship, cultural producers learned to market, negotiate, fundraise, write project applications, co-operate with foreign embassies and cultural centres, seek international partners and test their own entrepreneurial talent.

But festivals turned out to be a vulnerable part of the cultural infrastructure, quick to collapse in the new circumstances, be defunded, lose credibility and the support of peers, or to be written off summarily as a relic of the past regimes' representational politics. Fortunately, a whole generation of new festivals emerged quickly, driven by the energy of experienced state officials who finally could act as their own bosses or find the patronage of new democratically elected politicians. A new generation of young cultural professionals, who hardly had the time to experience the stifling impact of the public cultural institutions under socialism and who did not want to waste time by seeking to turn around old tired institutions, rushed to establish instead their own autonomous initiatives in a quickly emerging non-governmental cultural realm. From this pulsating field came new festival initiatives that throughout the 1990s changed the festival map of Europe, adding hundreds of new festivals of different kinds, also in places that were not previously perceived as *bona fide* festival cities. Festivals were created to celebrate the newly discovered freedoms, the joy of spontaneous sociability, the stunning diversity of cultural ideas, plans and aspirations, the spirit of dialogue, and even more of debate and polemic, the confrontation with previously unknown artistic forms, aesthetic choices and manners of communication.

Throughout the 1990s across Europe there was a surge in artistic ambitions and collaborative élan, very much driven and facilitated by festivals, despite the fact that neither the public authorities, nor the European Union, private foundations and commercial sponsors could supply the resources to respond to such new demand. Many new festival initiatives thus disappeared after a few pioneer editions, while others were picked up and consolidated by the engagement of municipal and regional authorities or, in Central and Eastern Europe, supported by the Open Society Institute network of foundations and cultural funding programmes. As cultural initiatives, networks and their membership grew and festivals proliferated, the superficial discourse of Europe was often invoked to mask underlying opportunism and imitative behaviour, lack of creativity and funding-driven concepts of festivals. Festival pathology became a steady part of the expanding festival scene and included a growing body of artistic work made specifically to fit the requirements, preferences and fashions of European festival circuits. Some festivals grew too fast and shifted from a primary concern with artistic issues into a money making mode, switched from non-profit to for-profit status, openly or tacitly, replacing the provision of a humble service to artists and audiences with self-aggrandizing promotion. The cultural industry, much enhanced by the digital revolution, especially with the internet boom after 1995, inserted its own models, templates, catchwords, slogans and marketing tricks into the festival business, but also diluted the meaning of festivals by softening essential differences and distinctive features, principles and values. In the name of the increasingly popular 'creative industries' oxymoron, fiestas, processions, parades, carnivals and other entertaining and money making crowd gathering schemes and events were thrown together with festivals driven by artistic visions and purposes.

There is no festival fatigue to discern, however, across Europe because cities are eager to enhance their own destination marketing, appeal to tourists and convention organisers, and to establish and market some kind of distinction in relation to hundreds of similar European cities, to promote themselves as pleasant, exciting, comfortable and prosperous places for investment, job creation and relocation by the creative classes. The popularity of festivals is generated by the dominance of the economic perspective on culture, seen not any longer for its inherent value and as an investment in the quality of citizenship and vibrancy of the community, but for its earning potential. Economic impact studies aim to convince funders and sponsors that festivals create significant economic benefits, boost consumption and expand employment. While new festival formulae abound (including new media; urban interventions; interdisciplinary, crossover pursuits; new thematic focuses on science, philosophy, economics and migration; monographic and commemorative festivals) the very notion of the festival has become quite problematic because it is used for any package of cultural events, condensed into two-three days, and endowed with a bombastic name, in the hope that the festival label will facilitate both fundraising and marketing. Consequently, continuously producing and programming cultural organisations are also launching their own festivals, to escape that deadly impression of business as usual, to create a sense of a special, extraordinary and unique cluster of events.

In the new millennium, festivals could be seen as a specific response to globalisation and its ambiguous cultural impact. However, many have become a matter of fashion, a trend to imitate and a cultural programming model to copy. At the same time, festivals – at least some festivals – function as strongholds of resistance to the standardising pressures of globalisation, as cultural interventions that seek to reinforce the specificity of a local place and establish their relationships with the world on their own terms, by nurturing co-operative ties with artists who share their critical stance and their rejection of readymade, stereotypical and standardized cultural commodities. Those festivals function not in a compensating and representational mode but in a developmental way, seeking to affirm specific artistic strategies and interests and to induce local developments with allies and collaborators brought in from elsewhere. In their best moments, such festivals articulate a productive dialectic of local and global.

Facets of festivals

Every large European city seems to be sliding from one festival to another all year round. Without any fear of saturation, moreover, and with a belief that for every festival type, sort, concept and theme there is an audience to be found, the endless merry go round of festivals spins at increasing speed across Europe, making the usage of the word festival increasingly arbitrary. A HP festival turns out to be a promotional campaign to unload older models of Hewlett Packard printers for a discount price. *Leiden Festival* is a student recruitment event at Leiden University. *Bijenkorf Festival* is a large sale in the Dutch department store. *Oysters Festival* is a joint promotion by several restaurants offering oyster based menus.

Setting the framework

To this extended notion of a festival one should add a mixed bag of affiliate phenomena, such as parades, processions, fiestas, carnivals, all mass events that have a certain, even if vague cultural component. Regardless of their specific value and merit, such events are not a subject of this book. Also, commercial festivals have been left on purpose outside the focus of the EFRP process since their for-profit orientation qualifies their artistic choices and limits their cultural impact.

Another festival category, consciously left out from this research process, is community celebrations, especially various festive events organised by specific ethnic, cultural, religious and linguistic minorities in Europe in order to assert their own presence in public space, to reinforce their own sense of collective identity and to pass it on to the next generation. Often associated with migration, such festivals seek to display and highlight some cultural markers of the group, from costumes to handicrafts, from folk dances to cuisine, and thus have some cultural meaning, at least in the broader anthropological conceptualisation of culture, but not always with a clear artistic dimension. The artistic aspect, to the extent that it is recognisable at all, is chiefly traditional, folkloristic and often amateur, perpetuating a certain narrow set of historic artistic forms, primarily for their linkage with the group identity and not for their artistic achievement per se. The artistic component is shaped as an invocation of group tradition, not as an opportunity for individual or collective creative innovation.

Beside those group festivals that seek to increase visibility for that group or community in the wider 'opaque' multicultural society, there are local celebrations of a village or an urban neighbourhood that also reinforce some group identity and the association of local residents to their territory, that during such festivals appears as a symbolically marked, embellished and ambitiously decorated space. The artistic dimension is here again subservient to the notion of the territory, its history, transformation, emblematic events in the collective memory and residents´ sense of pride about their belonging to such a place.

Seeking to shape a feasible and sustainable research framework for a systematic investigation of festivals and their rapid proliferation, EFRP deliberately limited its scope to those festivals in Europe, which are driven by an *artistic* vision, implemented through *international* programming, and carried out with the support of *public authorities*. The centrality of an artistic vision is what gives the festival its specificity, identity, cultural value. While some artistic festivals deliberately chose to limit themselves to a certain territory, city, region or country, in a research process that seeks to identify the Europe-wide trends and developments, the international component of festival programming is essential. EFRP's starting premise is that international outreach serves to specify and affirm the artistic dimension and at the same time produces a range of cultural and political impacts linked to the conceptualisation of Europe as an integrated, polyphonic cultural space. The EFRP project also focuses on festivals which explore perceptions of the cultural facets of European integration, the exercise of artistic mobility and cross-border cultural co-operation. With artistic ambitions at the centre of both its operating philosophy and international dimension of programming, a festival can be sustainable only if it receives some public support since its earning potential is obviously quite limited and expenditure high. Therefore, the third key factor in the EFRP conceptualisation of festival research is the role of public authorities, which links the festival phenomenon to the dynamics and sophistication of cultural policy, as conceptualised and carried out by municipal, regional or national governments and their funding agencies.

Shifts of function

Many of the artistic festivals that were set up in Europe after World War Two were endowed with a compensatory function – aiming to offer the public of a city or region some worthy artistic achievements that their regular cultural infrastructure could not produce or were otherwise limited features of a cultural season or the entire year. Festivals were at that time rare, exceptional and endowed with special prestige because they featured famous international artists who would otherwise not perform or have their work presented to these audiences. With the proliferation of festivals and increased artistic mobility, the competition among festival programmers grew. At the same time, festivals were established for the celebration of artistic excellence and expected to float above politics and its conflicts, tensions and clashing interests. Therefore, in the 1960s and 1970 many festivals served principally as platforms to promote and celebrate artistic excellence and cared little for other sorts of possible impact, economic, cultural or educational. Today, with innumerable festivals of all sorts and types crowding the cultural map of Europe, the best festivals find their distinction through being committed to delivering a *developmental* role, primarily in relation to their artistic discipline and to artistic innovation within it, but also in their commitment to nurturing young talent and to audience development. In a broader sense as well, festivals can be seen as pioneers, innovators and experimenters in the contemporary cultural practices of production, presentation and dissemination, as cultural players which because of their special status and intensive short lasting character tend to take more risks than continuously operating cultural institutions habitually do.

The main function of artistic festivals from our actual point of view is the generation of artistic and cultural effects that are invoked as a rationale for public subsidy. Increasingly, the expectation of public funders and consequently the attention of researchers and the media are shifting to examine levels of civic participation and social cohesion achieved by the artistic festivals within their local communities. The economic benefits of artistic festivals are often being invoked or even claimed as an argument for public support. Studies are being commissioned in order to prove and assess the impacts of a festival on the local economy and its value for the destination marketing of the local tourist offer. These studies are often rather unconvincing or based on an arbitrary methodology but indicate nevertheless to what extent economic reasoning has become widespread, if not central to the conceptualisation and implementation of cultural policy and in the configuration of its agenda and priorities.

As a discursive framework, festivals are able to sustain a complex relationship between their artistic and cultural discourses on the one hand and their more civic impacts on the other e.g. participation, social cohesion, economic arguments, concepts and data. These discourses do not run harmoniously nor do they necessarily reinforce each other and the festival managers themselves tend to use different arguments in communication with different interests (artists, the media, politicians).

Longevity

Artistic festivals come and go. Many succeed in achieving a respectable age, reappearing year after year, for several decades, and becoming a steady feature of the cultural constellation of a place, for at least at some specific time in the year. Other festival initiatives disappear after one or a few years, usually because they have lost public support. Behind a decision to disinvest from a festival there are usually organisational, conceptual, programming and management issues and failures. The long lasting festivals have prompted applications of cycle theory to explain their phasing, growth and changes. An analysis of defunct festivals reveals a pattern of troubles that undermine a festival operation, the pitfalls of routine and institutional fatigue and, in some cases, external troubles with fatal consequences, such as abrupt shifts in the funding policy of public authorities after an election, the change of politicians in key positions, and the imposition of severe budgetary restraints - any of which can result in the collapse of a festival operation.

One off festivals

Some festivals are especially initiated by public authorities themselves for some celebratory or commemorative purpose, without any ambition to run subsequent annual editions. In 2005, the celebrations of the 60th anniversary of the end of World War Two prompted a series of patriotic festivals in Russia that sought to glorify the USSR's military triumph over Nazi Germany and yield some political benefits for the present day Russian government, by providing moral and historic legitimisation. Many commemorative festivals appear in the year celebrating the anniversary of the birth or death of some prominent European artist, such as Mozart's 250th anniversary in 2006. Even Darwin's bicentenary and the 150 years from the publication of his *On the Origin of Species* prompted the organisation of several festivals in 2009, many of which were run by museums, universities and learned societies.

One off festivals are becoming quite common, regardless of any commemorative peg. A great number of cultural programmers prefer to package several events in a dense schedule, tied to a single weekend, and endow it with a bombastic festival name, in order to facilitate both fundraising and marketing. Increasingly, cultural organisations that produce continuously throughout the year or cultural season are choosing to launch festivals on their own, in order to create a sense of business *not* as usual, and to seek to appeal to audiences that will hopefully be attracted by a sense of something special, unique and unrepeatable being offered. "If I want to attract a large number of young spectators, I have to programme several festivals throughout my season", The director of the Maastricht Theatre, Theater aan het Vrijthof, admits candidly, but he adds, "if I want to programme some prominent artists in my season, I have to bring them within an invented festival formula because only in this way can I hope to acquire the extra funds needed to pay for them - either in the form of additional subsidy or sponsorship".

Mega-festivals

If those festivals that last only one weekend, reoccurring or not, are the minimalist version of the phenomenon, at the other extreme one finds festivals that stretch for weeks or months and function as a special season. Such is the *Festival d'Automne à Paris* and for some prolonged programming series such as this one begins to question whether they relate to the festival phenomenon or not. Another example is *Polska! Year*, a large programme of Polish culture that was organised with funding from the Polish government by the Adam Mickiewicz Institute in the United Kingdom from September 2009 to May 2010. This programme was designed in cooperation with many UK cultural organisations and in several cities, which served as hosts and partners. A festival? Probably not but another example of a format derived from festival practice.

The European Capital of Culture is a programme of the European Union nowadays selects two cities each year from different members states, exceptionally nine cities were designated in 2000 and three in 2010 (Essen/Ruhr, Pécs and Istanbul). Designated cities create a massive cultural programme, lasting over eleven months, a mega-festival of a sort that both tends to overestimate the willingness of many outside visitors to travel in order to partake in the programme and the capacity of the local residents to absorb and participate in such a programme, especially in smaller cities. In addition, such prolonged programmes may seriously stretch the stamina of the teams of professionals and volunteers that prepare them and run them.

Specifying the profile

Festivals come in many different forms. After World War Two many festivals sought to offer a multidisciplinary programme (e.g. *Edinburgh International Festival* and *Holland Festival*) or stuck to a single art form, most commonly classical music.

Multidisciplinary festivals aimed to attract and mix several distinct artistic audiences but sometimes attracted criticism from those who felt that their artistic affinities were downplayed in the programme to the advantage of some other artistic disciplines. With increased numbers of festivals and increased competition, a move towards specialisation has ensued. The panoply of music festivals includes all music idioms, specific formats (string quartets), genres (opera), periods (baroque, renaissance), instruments (piano, guitar) but unfortunately most classical music festivals play the same music one hears in most concert halls across Europe throughout the normal season — European symphonic and chamber music from Handel to Stravinsky, a rather limited repertory from only 200 years of music production. Contemporary composed music is supported and programmed by only a small number of niche festivals (e.g. Ars Musica, Belgium; *Huddersfield Contemporary Music Festival*, UK) which are therefore essential for the commissioning, production, publication and dissemination of such new works.

Similar specialisation exists in film: against well known and lesser known festivals of feature films, that attract much media coverage and orchestrate the distribution flows of newly produced works, there are a great many small niche festivals that feature films on anthropology, ecology, human rights (in some cases in co-production with Amnesty International), films for children, animated films, dance and music films, films on nature and the animal world and a category which is growing in popularity, the documentary film festival. Many of these have developed from a niche framework and acquired a rather large following, to some extent aided by the support coming from internet distribution and from the growing number of TV stations.

Theatre festivals have expanded from a narrow range of dramatic theatre to include other stage forms, and indeed the entire diffuse area of the performing arts. International theatre festivals in the past focused on the most prominent dramatic ensembles from abroad and featured productions of classic plays that belonged to a European canon of dramatic literature. Such canonical corpus of plays cannot be assumed any longer in Europe, and most performing arts festivals feature much self-conceived work, ranging from solo performance to rather complex productions with large numbers of participants, done on the stage of a conventional venue or on some found and appropriated location. If necessary, some sort of translation is provided from the language of production to the local language (or to English).

Increasingly, festivals claim an interdisciplinary orientation or cross over labels, suggesting that artistic works combine or merge various artistic disciplines. These claims are often not really substantiated but successful combinations, fusions and connections do occur, especially in the application of digital technology to dance and music creation and performance. Moreover, some festivals profile themselves in a thematic sense, by highlighting an intellectual topic or discipline each year.

Here festivals of science, history and memory, economy, food and philosophy should be mentioned but also those dedicated to globalisation, emigration, the human body... A diverse range of artistic work is used in these festivals to highlight and prompt a deliberative and intellectual dimension of the event: performance, film screening, exhibits and installations are combined with lectures, panels, debates and workshops. With rapidly increasing popularity these festivals are capable of mobilising a rather broad constituency of interest and in some cases place a festival-like artistic core within a congress-convention-exhibit-fair context.

Complex theming

Festivals are perceived as a convenient vehicle to advance a certain social and political agenda; hence festivals with a prominent feminist or gay banner, where again artistic components reinforce the discursive aspects. With the growing concern about climate change and its dismal prospects, it is not difficult to assume that festivals with environmentalist and ecological themes will become more frequent and more ambitious, combining artistic work, debate, political mobilisation and learning.

Literature and poetry festivals aim to counter the decline in reading habits and prompt more book buying and reading by organising attractive forms of presentation of literary works. They are an amalgamation and an expansion of traditional literary 'meet the author' sessions that libraries and bookshops programme regularly hold, but which are here blown up to huge proportions, with dozens of authors, critics, translators and editors brought together for a few days, in a fast flow of sessions, interviews, readings, writing workshops and debates.

Festivals with reoccurring yearly editions tend to distinguish them by using special themes, accents or slogans, more often derived *a posteriori*, from the selection made, than taken as an initial programming objective and selection framework. Quite common is a special emphasis in the programme to one geographic or cultural area, usually more distant and lesser known, from which several works are invited and presented. An artistic personality is in some cases especially honoured with several works presented, as when *Holland Festival* focused on Pina Bausch, Jiří Kylian, Francis Poulenc and Arvo Pärt in recent years. Since 2004 *Avignon Festival* has featured one or two artists every year as guests of honour whose work marks the connecting thread of the annual programme and who also acts as a co-programmer with the festival directors, initiating new creations among close colleagues and associates for inclusion in the festival (Thomas Ostermeier, Jan Fabre, Josef Nadj…).

Biennales and other exhibitions in the field of the visual arts, design and architecture are undergoing a visible festivalisation. They are taking over some of the features of festivals in order to enrich the basic offering which is an exhibition. Historically, this trend was pioneered by the *Biennale di Venezia*, the oldest biennale, which added a film festival in 1932 and after the war enlarged its formula to include theatre, dance and music programming. Nowadays, the *Biennale of visual arts* alternates with a *Biennale of architecture* and both contain accompanying artistic programmes within dense schedules, making them similar to a festival. In 2009, the *International Architecture Biennale* in Rotterdam included among other features, a film festival, dedicated to the US urban critic Jane Jacobs .

With this advanced differentiation of festival formulae it is very difficult to make any generalisation about festivals´ scope and focus. However, we can conclude that a quest for interdisciplinarity, a high degree of specialisation in the chosen art discipline, and usage of festival templates to address socio-political and intellectual issues are the main contemporary trends.

Programming Strategies

Most festivals seek to offer one coherent and condensed programme, but in the world of feature film festivals, where commercial interests tend to prevail and the availability of new productions is large, it is common to introduce several programme series that run in parallel during the festival, in addition to the main, 'official' programme. Those performing arts festivals that at some point decide to launch an 'off' or 'alternative' programme are probably seeking to demonstrate their openness to new/young talent and experimental tendencies, to be featured alongside established and more prestigious work, but run the risk of being accused of paternalism. Moreover, there is an inherent risk with several programme series or packages of diffusing media attention and fragmenting the interest of the audience – although there is also a chance of attracting an extended, additional audience.

The *Golden Mask* festival in Moscow emerged at the end of the 1990s as the major Russian festival of the performing arts, bringing to the capital the best theatre, dance and opera work, even from far away Russian cities that had become quite isolated as artistic mobility practically disappeared after the collapse of the USSR. To this programme the *Golden Mask* added a Russian showcase of work by new, emerging groups. A series of discoveries and tentative new developments in the Russian performing arts, created by small groups that were usually overwhelmed and marginalised by larger repertory ensembles, quickly attracted more than 100 foreign critics, dramaturgs, theatre directors, programmers and presenters, curious to take a look at an unknown part of the Russian cultural scene.

Programme selection and coherence

Festival professionals are not very talkative when asked about their own programming methods and strategies. They stress curiosity, perseverance, and willingness to travel a lot and to take considerable risks in their programming choices. Music and film festival directors can rely on being able to access digital material mailed to them but performing arts festival programmers depend on the numerous trips they must make after meticulous research. Programming without a serious travel budget can be limiting and dangerous since DVDs offer often a distorted idea of what a production is all about. Those who cannot afford a decent travel budget are forced to programme on the basis of rumour, gossip and second hand information, hardly reliable, or to draw from the artistic offer in their vicinity.

Programmers like to explore a specific geographic area and a distinct cultural realm, and highlight it in the programme, or to identify and emphasise some thematic or conceptual line that interconnects individual artistic works featured in the festival. Every better known international festival is inundated with offers by producers and agents. Larger festivals can maintain professional research staff to track ongoing artistic events, especially premieres of new productions, browse print and digital information sources and highlight what the programmer should be seeing by making a trip.

In programming, festival professionals are usually led by their own interests, affinities and intuitions. A personal network of informal advisors and colleagues is also important. However, someone who operates on the basis of such signals only risks producing a festival that suffers from an excessive topsy-turvy quality. More experienced and better resourced/endowed festival directors seek a clear-cut programming line, a synthesis, a confrontation, or to affirm some new emerging orientation or tendency. But to be able to reveal it in their programme they have to see a lot of productions, many of them in vain. Professional vanity also plays a role because everyone would like to be acknowledged for a surprising discovery, for presenting some remarkable artistic work, previously unknown or unnoticed. With the proliferation of festivals, this is becoming a difficult ambition to satisfy.

Complaints that festivals of similar profile and artistic discipline excessively resemble each other because they offer more or less the same programme are quite common but not necessarily justifiable. Festival directors and critics hopscotch from one festival to another and thus risk seeing more or less the same highlights, but the audiences are less mobile and thus it does not matter for a local public that the same artistic work has appeared elsewhere, at some other festival, as long as the work is in itself appropriately provoking or exciting.

Most festivals are programmed by one person, exceptionally by a duo that work together effectively due to being complementary in interests and affinities. Programming by a committee risks producing a disjointed and excessively heterogeneous festival. There are also opportunistic entrapments: going after some artistic work because of its publicity potential rather than artistic merit, or inviting some work because it could be assumed that some private or public party will pay for it, or because a sponsor will be easy to recruit, following fads and fashionable features ... these are all rather common festival programming sins, easy to spot by professional observers.

A special case of opportunism are those pseudo-European festivals that claim that they present in every edition the culture and artistic output of another country, thus waving a colourful tapestry of ongoing artistic productions in Europe, while in fact they aim to secure, every time, funding to do so from another promotion-hungry ministry or government agency. The following year, the supposed cultural discoveries are quietly set aside and another cultural realm is featured prominently, not so much because of its value and specificities but because of the availability of new governmental funds. Such opportunistic festival directors operate in synergy with the opportunistic public authorities that are willing to buy exposure and passing prominence for themselves.

Monographic festivals seemingly present a less daunting task, by focusing on the oeuvre of a single artist. An international Shakespeare or Chekhov or Ibsen festival does not suffer from any lack of new artistic creations available, inspired to a degree by the plays of one of those authors. In music, however, a focus on the oeuvre of one composer, even if very prolific, such as Mozart or Handel or Rossini, could create problems, especially after several yearly editions, and require some stretching of the rigid monographic formula, by inclusion of a composer's contemporaries and followers.

Programming integrity

Festival directors earn their professional reputations by the coherence of their concepts and how they are translated into a concrete festival selection, resulting from the diligence of their research and their critical scrutiny of the artistic work available. Most importantly, they earn their credibility through the loyalty, personal attention and generosity displayed to the artists and the artistic collectives they host. Respect for the artistic process, the framing of the artistic work in the festival presentation, the discursive context created to facilitate its reception, the quality of hospitality: these are the most important elements that contribute to someone's professional standing, reputation and respect as a festival director. The narcissism, arrogance, superficiality and opportunism of a festival director can quickly throw a shadow on the entire festival and taint its reputation within the international artistic community. Bad hospitality, sloppiness in financial matters, and delayed payments have ruined the reputations of quite a few festivals and discredited their directors. Thus integrity of programming needs to be backed up by similar integrity in presentation, management and hosting.

Festivals as producers

Increasingly, music and performing arts festivals go beyond the programming of previously created work and embark on producing or co-producing new work themselves. It has almost become a matter of prestige that an ambitious festival shares a producer, or more often a co-producer, with other festivals and venues. The ambition is to create and feature new artistic work, previously unseen, also to make it possible for selected and especially trusted and appreciated artists to work together, which would be practically impossible outside of the context of a festival. Festivals frequently use international co-producing consortia in order to raise resources needed for the creation of the new work, to share risks that are inherent in such creation, and to increase the visibility and the shelf life of the new work by guarantying a larger number of performances among the co-producing partners, in an expectation that this exposure will attract other programmers who will select the work for their own venues and festivals at some later point. In practice, festivals and venue programmers are brought together through a shared appreciation of an artist or artistic collective and an eagerness to facilitate its new creative endeavour. Most co-producing consortia do not go beyond a shared financial input, but in some cases this could involve a complex combination of resources, services, responsibilities and tasks, coordinated to guarantee the effectiveness and efficiency of the creative process. One of the partners usually acts as the executive producer and manages the process through to the premiere, keeping the other partners in the loop.

International co-producing consortia lift international cultural co-operation to a higher level of complexity. In a multilateral setting, the risks of misunderstanding and incompatibility increase but so do the learning opportunities and potential synergetic effects. Consortia function well if the partners are mutually compatible and if they know each other well, so that they embark on a co-production with some mutual trust as a starting point. Usually, they belong to diverse national cultural systems, so that each has a specific relationship with its own public authorities as key funders and with specific sets of responsibilities, strategic concerns and obligations that need to be recognised and understood by the other partners. Despite increasing artistic mobility in Europe and the growth of the practice of co-production, partners are aware that they operate within different sets of professional standards and routines, against a background of divergent national traditions and institutional typologies. For festivals, co-productions are a method to deepen their relationship with much appreciated artists (i.e. they may have been featured previously in the festival programme), in order to create the added value of a new production for their audiences. The risks of course are considerable because the prospect of artistic failure is ever present in such a process. But festivals are essentially risk taking initiatives and the best among them have it hard wired into their DNA to probe the limits of the possible and feasible.

Educational and outreach programmes

Every ambitious festival nowadays seeks to develop a rich panoply of adjacent activities to support, enlighten and reflect upon the features of its core programme. Educational and outreach activities are becoming an area of experimentation and rapid development. Education activities can be focused on discrete groups, from small children to teenagers, and also on adult audiences and senior citizens. Conventionally, educational activities have been limited to not much more than meetings with artists. This is now changing, especially in those countries where public subsidies for culture are linked to some expected educational benefits those cultural activities should produce. The difficulty for many festivals is that they see themselves primarily as an artistic project, encumbered with logistical challenges, great time pressures, hospitality contingencies and budgetary constraints. In this context educational activities may be perceived by festival leaders or festival staff members as a luxury, a nuisance, an additional burden. Others see these activities as a way to legitimise, at least in a formal manner, public subsidy and to earn some goodwill but not necessarily as an investment in the future, and in the development of a more discriminating public.

In more ambitious cases, educational activities are initiated months before the festival takes place, with specific, well targeted groups of children or young people, in the form of a complex hands-on project that may be developed in school or post-school time and with the climax occurring within the festival, where it will stand related to some major feature of the festival programme. At the core of this approach is the belief that learning by doing works much better with educational groups than learning about some artistic form and working through lectures and discussions. Such ambitious engagement is possible only if the festival selection is known months in advance, if the festival can afford to employ professional educational staff and if it can identify some schools where there will be enough ambition and goodwill to cooperate in a rather prolonged time sequence. Through this hands-on experience, it is hoped that participants in education projects will develop an understanding of the creative process and not just of an artistic event, to learn new skills and how to draw on/develop their own imagination and talent, and also to receive recognition for the entire effort when they present their final work as part of the festival itself.

For adults too, educational programmes can start before the festival and then peak during its run. The greying of Europe, the massive post-World War Two baby boom generation now turning into senior citizens, requires from festivals – and all cultural practitioners - to expand their educational programmes for adults and think of special programmes for senior citizens. This is not only because they are becoming a large population group but also because they retire quite early, possess much free time, considerable levels of education and often pronounced cultural interests which they can finally pursue with energy and loyalty in their retirement.

Dance festivals, for instance, offer an opportunity to bridge the gap between professionals and amateurs. *Holland Dance Festival* in The Hague offers amateurs, in parallel with its artistic programme, a range of workshops and master classes in various dance idioms and an additional set of workshops for dance teachers who give lessons to children, youth and adults, not just in ballet and contemporary dance but in popular dance forms as well. The entire effort is based on the assumption that people who practice an art form at whatever level of competence may develop a depth of interest that will make them a loyal part of the audience. And yet, such efforts are quite rare in the entire range of music festivals where, it seems, the boundary between professionals and amateurs seems to be sharply drawn and jealously guarded.

Outreach could be seen as a specific effort to engage potential audience groups that are not yet part of the regular festival public. It is an effort not only to expand but to diversify the festival audience. Again, outreach programmes might be seen as just a formal, minimal effort to counter the elitism charges that are often directed at festivals and to demonstrate some principled commitment to inclusiveness and cultural diversity. To succeed and yield some lasting results, outreach programmes need to be conceived with much ambition and sophistication, initiated early, pursued with stamina and carefully evaluated and adjusted. It is virtually impossible for a festival as a 'here today, gone tomorrow' sort of organisation, a temporary affair with a working process of great intensity, packaged in a condensed time frame, to carry out such outreach activities alone. To be effective in delivering outreach work a festival requires strong partnerships with those organisations, public or NGO, that work continuously with culturally marginalised and socio-economically underprivileged social groups.

Professional training

Only recently have festivals begun to include in their programmes of educational work separate opportunities for professionals, in addition to what they do for the public. Professionals of course have specific needs, aspirations and expectations and it is becoming common for a festival to organise workshops and master classes for young professionals.

These opportunities enable them to develop their professional expertise, and to profit from working with the major artists engaged within the festival programmes. Workshops for young critics, advancing their discursive and analytical capacities, have also become more common, as well as training for producers and managers in international cultural co-operation.

Festivals are also convenient occasions to use the concentration of professionals, attending a festival, to launch a debate and engage in reflection, which may otherwise be difficult to fit into the busy schedule of artists and the dynamic of artistic processes. Since festivals attract media attention, such professional debates are convenient for agenda setting and advocacy aimed at the public authorities. *Avignon Festival* has become a privileged platform for a whole series of professional encounters, taking place every summer during the three week long run of the festival, and set up by a range of cultural organisations, from France and other European countries.

Prizes

Most festival programmers resent juries and prizes and consider them an anachronistic feature of the festival business, an almost debasing arrangement. The more conceptual festival programming becomes, the more it moves away from the notion of an artistic competition where the prizes seek to establish, confirm or reverse an artistic hierarchy. The rejection of prizes reflects the stance that each artistic work selected for a festival programme stands on its own merit and that awarding prizes would violate such specificity. In some countries, however, awards are still very important and laureates draw some lasting benefits from them. Official juries are in some cases supplemented by juries of critics and in some festivals the audience awards its own prize by vote as well. Alternatively prizes may be seen as a way to attract a sponsor who then endows the prize with their own name and some cash. In film festivals, that influence distribution, prizes are much coveted attributes, regularly invoked in film marketing as proof of success. The intrigues around the jury composition and its deliberations, the attempts to influence jury members, the gossip, recriminations and ensuing polemics about the prizes awarded may be seen as part of the festival folklore and, a bit more seriously, as its functional capacity to sort out values and reputations, with more or less authority and contestation.

The primacy of programming

Programming is the most delicate and most important task for a festival. It endows the festival with its function and specific position, interprets the conditions in an artistic discipline and highlights trends and tendencies within it, inevitably from the individual prism of the programmer and reflecting his/her idiosyncrasies and obsessions. It is a conceptual activity that rests on a delicate operation of de-contextualisation of the selected work of art from its original setting and re-contextualisation in the festival programme. The rest is logistic and communication, hospitality, fundraising and accounting, all functions and tasks of a much more pragmatic nature, carried out in order to make the programming rationale and selected works featured in the programme understandable, well presented and appreciated.

The space of festivals

This essay considers the spatial dimension of festival activities, both in the city and in the countryside, the variants of the site used and the importance of the spatial context and a festival's impact upon it.

Urban festivals

There is some debate about whether it is better for festivals to be concentrated in one place or dispersed in a larger urban zone. If all festival activities are concentrated in one space, a congress centre, a theatre venue, a concert hall, this can serve as a social hub for the festival, a place of socialisation, where participants will more easily be able to switch from one programme feature to another, without wasting time. Such a feature also facilitates sharing time socially and in meetings with their family, friends, colleagues; plus the press and media have all the people they need in the same place, artists, public and journalists.

The opposite argument is that dispersion makes festivals more visible and enlarges their impact because festival activities pop up at various locations across the city, invoke and involve several local neighbourhoods and thus make it easier for local residents to notice and embrace the festival, even if some festival visitors have a journey to make from one location to another. The social and economic impact of the festival is expanded and therefore experienced in more places and thus there is some fairness and equality in dispersion. The decision to decentralise festival activities to dispersed points is not driven by practical considerations only but also by political contingencies: to seek to move away from the centre of the city, the traditional hub of most cultural activities, away from the prominent cultural institutions, endowed by tradition and prestige, in order to reach the peripheral or underprivileged neighbourhoods signals a determination to escape from elitist entrapments and to extend the impact of the festival into the cultural, social and economic life of those urban zones that are by and large deprived of much cultural activity, especially of a festive and international nature.

Ambitious festival programmes with several programme series or several performances or concerts or screening each day might not be able to squeeze into one venue alone, even a quite big one, and thus need to opt for dispersal. In a big city this may result in some travel time between the programme units and additional logistic fine tuning and schedule adjustment. In small towns, switching from one venue to another could be a matter of minutes but in a small place the presence of the festival is felt all over anyhow. For some music, theatre, dance and film festivals a venue is a necessity, whether one or several are used, concentrated in one zone or dispersed across several. Venue-centred festivals in the performing arts might include one or several productions that do not fit a venue and require a specific adjusted ambiance. Some festivals specialise in ambient theatre, dance and music and seek a variety of appropriate sites to show their selection, investing a great deal of imagination and logistic resources in assuring appropriate and inspiring sites.

Increasingly, the city and its dynamics, and the experience of urbanity, have become subject matters for the festivals themselves. A new generation of festivals seeks to explore the implicit texture of urban spaces, to reclaim and revitalise its public zones, especially those left to neglect and decay and those exposed to corporate encroachment, intrusive and ubiquitous advertising, obsessive surveillance and paranoid security regimes. The artistic programmes of those festivals could be described as urban interventions, in some cases offering unexpected guerrilla-style performances or installations that aim to cause a sensation of estrangement, to disrupt the habitual perceptive patterns of passers-by, alter their standard routes and enliven their experience of negotiating the public space of the city with surprising, even provocative encounters.

Such interventions include artistic lighting of buildings, projections of images onto the facades, erection of temporary structures, special decorations, marking of new routes and pathways, placing of billboards with artistic work (especially photography) opening up of some buildings that are usually inaccessible to the public, and the generation of unexpected frequency and flows of movement of large numbers of people through the use of SMS (short message service) and Twitter. The concentration of people into urban places that are usually almost empty or used only for rapid, low-frequency transition creates new temporary hubs of sociability. All those strategies, together with the dispersal patterns engineered by the festivals, alter the mental maps most citizens have of their own city and re-arrange the established hierarchy of specific sectors as zones of interest, fun, buzz and appealing sociability. At the same time, some zones - habitually perceived as boring, culturally irrelevant or even dangerous - are revealed in some more attractive features.

While the creative city concept, as popularised by Charles Landry[11] and Richard Florida[12], has become a catchword, pursued by politicians, real estate developers and some cultural operators, with more or less opportunism and manipulation, festivals demonstrate their capacity to contribute to urban revitalisation processes but at the same time to serve as platforms for critical reflection, and even subversion. By exposing particular interests involved in urban regeneration, by pointing out the winners and losers and by empowering the micro-infrastructure of civil society to act as the subject of these complex, long-term processes and not as passive observers and consumers only, festivals affirm their democratic, mobilising and critical potential to fuse artistic creativity and public debate.

Rural festivals

Although festivals are mainly associated with cities and placed within an urban cultural scene, the number of rural festivals seems to be growing, even if we consider only those events with a clear artistic primary purpose and international

[11] Landry, C. The Creative City, London: Earthscan, 2000.
[12] Florida, R. The Rise of the Creative Class: And how it's transforming work, leisure, community and everyday life, New York: Perseus Book Group, 2002.

71

dimension, and leave aside various village celebrations that are inspired mainly by the desire to preserve and revive local traditions and even more by the ambition to attract tourists. Rural artistic festivals rest on the premise that tourists do not want to spend their vacation in a cultural desert, but may wish to pursue their interests even while vacationing, and that nearby urban dwellers might be prompted to make a short excursion to the rural area if they have an additional motivation, provided by the artistic attraction of a festival. Of course, rural festivals have to deal with some inherent restraints, such as the low density of population in the rural areas, access to accommodation and facilities that can provide for the comfort requirements of visitors, as well as limitations in the specific cultural infrastructure available in the area.

Nevertheless, countryside areas are appropriated as festival sites, and churches, monasteries, castles or their ruins become festival hubs, as well as village squares, parks and shores of rivers and lakes. Festival organisers in rural areas hope, just as their colleagues who operate in smaller towns, that they will attract a more sophisticated tourist clientele, who may extend their stay and spend more money, but also that the festival will endow the area with some special distinction and affirm its unique features and qualities. The key resource and tacit ally is nature itself, its beauty, serenity and capacity to inspire and thus various forms of land art join theatre and dance performances and concerts. If a rural area possesses some valuable cultural historic object, it could become a key attraction point, a festival hub, a recognisable symbol of the festival, but this complements the core aim of such festival programmes which are to spread the beneficial impacts widely and to expand the festival habitat further into the natural environment and among villages and farms and the lives of local people and visitors.

The success of many rural festivals is dependent on the great goodwill invested by the local population, on their co-operative mentality and willingness to volunteer and offer hospitality in their homes, barns, and courtyards. In low density areas, that experience a dramatic increase in visitors during the summer months, the local infrastructure (especially roads, water supply, and electricity) can be heavily overloaded and demand some careful planning, special arrangements and redistribution to avoid system collapse. Commercial festivals, of rock and pop music for instance, that are driven by the profit motive, bring tens of thousands of visitors to rural areas who mostly camp in improvised camping areas for three or four days, create traffic jams on the narrow rural roads, overwhelm these areas with noise and leave behind a trace of garbage in trampled fields. For artistic, non-profit festivals in rural areas it is therefore most important to keep some sense of the scale, not to let the operation grow too rapidly and beyond the limits of sustainability, to respect nature and avoid damage through the sheer numbers and concentration of people in places that are serene and beautiful precisely because they are isolated and not much exposed to visitors.

With a growing environmentalist culture in Europe and concerns for the consequences of climate change, attitudes to nature are changing, even among urban dwellers. Nature is increasingly seen as a precarious and vulnerable resource to be handled with care and concern. Festival operators, and not only those in rural areas, are becoming conscious of the ecological footprint of their activity. They take measures to anticipate and limit the ecological damage that may be inflicted by the festival operation and even seek to undertake restorative actions that should help to repair any damage resulting from intensive exposure and stress during the festival. This presents artistic festivals with a great chance to develop a broad alliance with the ecological movement and to integrate an ecological consciousness in their operation, among artists, staff, volunteers and visitors. (The commercial music festival sector has made significant progress in this respect with the emergence of organisations such as GO Events, Julie's Bicycle and A Greener Festival which prioritise responsible, sustainable management practices.)

Festivals in rural areas rely on the local, small scale tourist infrastructure, mainly of family run accommodation, eateries, stores and other services. Small, unique and place specific is what visitors want. Therefore, festivals are becoming a convenient way of achieving discrete and sophisticated local product placement, not in overwhelming merchandising, kitsch souvenirs and phony handcrafts, usually made in China, but of high quality products that rely on local resources, skills and accumulated know how. The 'slow food' movement, for instance, as developed chiefly in Italy, is a most welcome accompaniment of the festivals' artistic offer with a range of organic food, health and cosmetic products.

Appropriated sites

In contrast to cultural objects and especially venues, appropriated festival sites are either cultural-historic objects (castles, churches, fortresses, convents, archaeological sites), or public spaces of daily usage (squares, plazas, streets, occasionally train stations and bus terminals), former industrial buildings, and sites of particular 'natural' interest. Each type imposes a certain regime of usage and some restraints in festival appropriation.

Many festivals are situated in heritage locations, such as the Court of Honour of the Pope's Palace in Avignon, the remains of the Greek Theatre in Epidaurus, the Roman Theatre in Orange, the Roman Arena in Pula (which has been used for film festival screenings), or the Alhambra in Granada. Such festivals appropriate these valuable places, which are usually visited throughout the year as architectural heritage sites, for specific artistic usage but the organisers need to develop a preservation/protection programme that will guarantee the safety of the site and which will cope with the large number of visitors the festival receives and the need to bring on site a large amount of technical equipment, bleachers and accompanying provisions for the comfort and safety of the visitors and artists. As festival sites, these cultural heritage locations are inspiring, sometimes even dramatic. Festivals place them in the centre of public and especially cultural interest and expand their exposure as artistic and social spaces, without necessarily achieving a deeper understanding by their visitors of the sites 'cultural-historic value', its creation, history and previous modes of usage.

By inserting contemporary creativity in a context shaped by the cultural, historic value of the object, festivals can stress and exploit the tension between cultural production in the past and the present, between tradition and innovation. The festival's artistic usage can break though the limited preservationist concerns and ideology that may determine the regime under which such objects are usually placed. International festivals can lift these objects from the confines of a local, regional or national history, culture and heritage and make them appreciated as objects of European cultural significance.

Memories to
Dragan Klaic

Kulturträger Dragan Klaic

Krzysztof Czyżewski

The Polish edition of Mobility of Imagination was the first book by Dragan Klaic published in Poland[13], although some of his articles and columns appeared in Polish periodicals and edited books. The modest amount of publications stands in contrast with the number of his friends, collaborators and disciples this indefatigable thinker, expert, lecturer and traveller had in Poland. The contrast is even bigger if we consider his imposing expertise in Polish culture concerning not only theatre, that he knew inside out, but also literature, history, Polish-Jewish relations, the traditions of the Parisian *Kultura*[14], KOR (Workers' Defence Committee) and

[13] Klaic, D. Mobilność wyobraźni. Międzynarodowa współpraca kulturalna, Warszawa 2011.
[14] *Kultura Paryska*, was a leading Polish-émigré literary-political magazine, published from 1947 to 2000 by Instytut Literacki (Literary Institute), initially in Rome, then in Paris.

Solidarity, and after 1989, his expertise in Poland's cultural as much as foreign policies.

Lublin was the only city candidate for the European Capital of Culture this expert on European projects came in close co-operation with, co-authoring its first applications. Still remembered today is the amazement of the city mayor during his first meetings with this Amsterdam-based expert who pointed out to him all the strong and weak points of the city, beginning with the Polish-Lithuanian Union, Western and Eastern influences along with the multicultural heritage, migrations of the population, historical disasters, the rich traditions of the universities and alternative theatre, concluding not only with a description of the current cultural infrastructure of the city but developing it to include a detailed analysis of Lublin's economic investment, demographic and geopolitical problems. This anecdote highlights not only Dragan Klaic's knowledge as such but the way he understood and practiced international cultural co-operation.

Mobility of Imagination[15] is one of those books whose content is as important as the author.

[15] Klaic, D. Mobility of imagination: A companion guide to international cultural cooperation, Budapest: CAC Central European University, 2007.

And as Dragan Klaic belongs to those reticent in speaking, least of all, writing about themselves, it seems worthwhile to examine the man behind this systematically ordered guide book for experts. All the more worthwhile that the success of international cultural co-operation depends on something more than just textbook type professionalism, even top quality one. This 'something' might seem elusive as it is apparently connected with interpersonal relations, authenticity and life experience of concrete people.

The value of cultural co-operation itself is indisputable nowadays. The world favours it and Europe constitutes a significant factor of integration; it is also aided by the mobility of our fluid contemporaneity and globalisation. It all seems obvious, but for its enthusiasts the difficulty lies in obtaining constantly refined tools and means of development. While considering it, it is also worthwhile remembering that the author of the *Mobility of Imagination* himself experienced the appalling consequences of the collapse of Yugoslavia and Tito's vision for a nation that occupied a common cultural space, one that integrated several nationalities and offered a common identity, language and a dense network of contacts, including artistic ones. The destructive and bloody break-up of Yugoslavia was a traumatic experience that left behind only physical and spiritual ruins and a disbelief in the value of other 'naive' projects, and which led some to develop a defeatist consent about life, enclosed within their national or other horizon-limiting perspectives. With Dragan Klaic it was different. His engagement in 'Europe as a cultural project' and his creation of alternative transnational platforms of co-operation in the world, benefitted from the intensity and total commitment of a man who knew very well the price of losing something precious and who had the knowledge of how easy it was to destroy the edifice of co-existence which had been constructed years before but which disappeared so very rapidly. Dragan Klaic understood very well that genuine cultural cooperation cannot be based on ideology, hypocrisy or coercion. One sensible lesson that can be learnt from the destruction of a bridge in a neighbourly conflict is the construction of a better, more solid bridge, because there is no other alternative. Therefrom stems the importance of the role of the teacher able to pass on the arcana of his craft, by others unnoticed, ignored or treated cursorily. And that is why Dragan Klaic's book is based on precision and meticulous approach to detail, wide and multi-faceted scrutiny, reference to what is concrete and experienced, dragging idealists back to earth and handing them the tools to work with. This post-Yugoslav citizen tells us between the lines that international cultural co-operation performed carelessly is something worse than just some bad or failed co-operation. It means yielding to the forces of parochialism, destruction and xenophobia, whose power feeds on nothing else but our nonfeasance, ineptitude and loss of vigilance towards the darker side of our nature.

In his autobiographical *Exercises in Exile*[16], Dragan Klaic's analysis of the vicissitudes of an emigrant's fate reveals that even in his childhood he was already getting ready for the role of an exile. The same may be said about his preparation for transborder cultural co-operation. As a man of culture who mastered the art of living far away from his native land, his situation may represent an important breeding ground for building a common cultural space for people of different languages and nationalities?

Sarajevo, Dragan Klaic's birthplace, is today a symbol of the tragedy of a mutlicultural community, the war waged against cosmopolitans, the citizens of *charshiya*, those favouring coexistence with the others instead of ethnic cleansing. He, of course, remembers a different Sarajevo, one that felt like home for his mother's family with their tangled

[16] Klaic, D. Exercises in Exile, Amsterdam: Cossee, 2004.

Jewish-Polish-Serbian roots. His grandmother turning to her grandson spoke with a Bosnian accent in her Serbo-Croat and would weave into their conversations various Polish words which he remembered his whole life. A similar story can be told about his father's family in Novi Sad, where he lived before he left to study and later settle in Belgrade. Here Hungarian and German were dominant languages, the latter replacing Yiddish, and of course the Voivodina accent of Serbo-Croat. Digging deeper into the family history, one could follow his ancestors wandering from Cracow to the Balkans, and others from the Habsburgian provinces that are now parts of Poland, Ukraine, Hungary and Romania. He would often underline the comfort his family felt living in the world of the Austro-Hungarian empire, moving freely across it in search of better prospects for work and living, changing languages and perfectly adapting themselves to the local neighbourhood, at the same time preserving the feeling of belonging to one and the same cultural *milieu*, so common among the Central Europeans.

I mentioned earlier the break-up of Yugoslavia as the experience of the collapse of the community building project that Dragan Klaic felt personally. And my short outline of Klaic's family history brings us to another tragic event in the history of modern Europe. Born in 1950, Dragan could only learn about the Holocaust second hand but his closest family bore witness to this shadow in his family's recent history. The 9th November 1990, the day he emigrated West from Yugoslavia, the first night spent in Vienna, recalled for him the memory of the 'Crystal Night', and in his case it was by no means just a loose association of the date from a history textbook. The tale he recreated later from the stories he heard and the fate of the members of his family, to a large extent refer to the idea of building a common project on the Central European borderlands whose capitals were Vienna, Prague, Budapest, Cracow or Czernowitz, a project in which many of the main protagonists were Jews. Not without good cause then, they were called *Kulturträger*, i.e. those who carry culture across national borders. A popular misconception identifies Jewish culture with enclosed city quarters, such as Josefov in Prague or Kazimierz in Cracow, whereas Jews were also co-founders of many cities' cosmopolitan agoras. The fact that their descendant writes today a guide to international cultural co-operation for Europeans is evidence of the continuity of a certain tradition. It is a wonderful one too, if we consider the fact that this continuity was not established on the foundations of a predictable and simple sequence of events, but was a persistently and miraculously salvaged and sustained belief in the need to oppose the dark forces of the advocates of the "final solution" or ethnic cleansing, and this despite his experience of a failure in the field.

An excellent foundation for developing his skills in cultural co-operation from his early childhood was Dragan Klaic's mastery of many languages. The languages of his Novi Sad family were Serbo-Croati, Hungarian and German. Still in his youth he mastered French, at that time still the main language of European culture. The language he used daily in Amsterdam was Dutch. He also knew Italian, Spanish, Slovenian and could read the Cyrillic script. But of particular importance in his life was English, the language he chose very early, long before his emigration, to be the medium of his profession. Also in English he defended his PhD thesis at Yale University. With the end of the Cold War, he started, together with his friend Dušan Jovanović, the theatrical quarterly *Euromaske*. The magazine's editorial offices were in Ljubljana but all the texts were published in English, a unique phenomenon in those times, attempting to cover with its range the whole of Europe. It is also significant that his autobiography, *Exercises in Exile*, was also written in English. Beginning his co-operation with Lublin, he alarmed the whole cultural milieu by demanding everybody should use English and informing the city authorities that either they sponsor intensive English courses for people in the city's cultural sector or they can forget the title of the European Capital of Culture.

So ardently cultivated by Dragan Klaic, citizenship of Europe was for him based, first of all, on the decisive role of the common language for intercultural competences, partner co-operation and integration. However, to be well adjusted to life in contemporary Europe one needs another level. It is that of a constant linguistic polyphony, transition from one language into another, to be able to cultivate local tongues and learn new ones, to simultaneously facilitate getting accustomed to changing your place of living, to the loss of the small homeland and settling into a new neighbourhood. If our imagination becomes, also thanks to the development of cultural co-operation, a mobile one, we have to match it with our linguistic competence; otherwise we won't be able to inhabit this world where 'while in exile we are home':

"...what once used to be home became distant, detached, even foreign and to some extent inaccessible. The notions of home and abroad went through a stern reappraisal. In order to carry it out with precision I needed to undertake several experimental journeys. In each of them I was not

going back but rather going away, to a destination that despite its certain familiarity has acquired some new features and labels. And with a home base once fixed in the Northwestern Europe, I ventured further in the Balkan region than ever before, making some surprising connections."[17]

What is striking in Dragan Klaic's words, like in many other fragments of *Exercises in Exile* is the surprisingly positive tone he uses to refer to the loss of home and exile that others usually remember as a catastrophe or a wound that would never heal. He inherited this tone from his ancestors, for whom emigration never had any negative connotations. In the worst circumstances it meant a just-in-time escape against an incoming disaster, often bringing better conditions of life and satisfying their curiosity about the world. However, there is more to the words of an exile, the experience of the fact that leaving home and journeying towards new horizons does not have to mean losing your roots. Distancing yourself offers an opportunity for deeper and more far-reaching returns to home places or, at least, constant creative dialogue with them. In other words, it is not permanent settlement but mobile imagination that makes the world our home.

[17] Klaic, D. Exercises in Exile, Amsterdam: Cossee, 2004. p.

Dragan Klaic, just like many other border-landers, found it difficult to define his identity and for a long time must have wondered how to fill the entry called 'nationality' or for that fact, other entries demanding that he stated where he belonged. Initially, i.e. around the mid-eighties the answer seemed straightforward and indisputable: Yugoslav. Later he would have said: European with a Dutch passport, but then which form could allow such a long answer and which government would allow so much ambiguity... Between the labels of 'Yugoslav' and 'European' stretches the space of one's life drama, intent on search, rebellion and strenuous effort to be at home in exile.

Mobility of Imagination is an important guide for all who wish to deal with international cultural co-operation. Such a guide remains Dragan Klaic himself, an emigrant finding a home in exile, a confirmed cosmopolitan and European. He experienced the loss of illusions and historical catastrophes and went on travelling, gathering friends around his IKEA table at Churchill-laan in Amsterdam and sending dozens of e-mails every day in different languages, engaging others in the building of a common cultural space, the only one that includes supranational citizenship.

Dragan Klaic passed away on 25 August 2011. He spent his last few months in and out of hospital, in

Amsterdam. In the beginning, there was nothing disturbing in it. It was a treatment which had been planned a long time in advance. At least that's what Dragan wanted his friends to believe. He wouldn't allow the smallest measure of self-pity and never said what troubled him. It was just, simply, that his somatic 'engine' was to be 'lubricated' so that he could go into action with renewed intensity. But his body, accustomed to titanic work, had required attention for a long time already. I remember how surprised I was when Rose Fenton managed to talk him into daily yoga exercise during Dragan's stay in my house in Krasnogruda – until then such 'spoiling oneself' had been regarded by him as an unacceptable waste of time. So, his friends perceived Dragan's stay in hospital as a break for some necessary treatment. But soon Dragan's e-mails changed their tone. They became shorter, perfunctory, deprived of his usual spark of engagement, and then ceased to arrive. One break from work that could appear in Dragan's creative life, this final, dividing one... I'm stopped halfway in finishing the sentence by the consistent agnosticism of the author of the *Exercises in Exile*, based on the morality claiming that all man's actions refer to 'here' and another human being, and never to 'there' and God.

But it's so hard to write 'he left us', or change the tense of the text to the past. He will remain with us as long as the memory of his presence remains alive, as long as we are determined to continue with the ideas, attitudes and paths we shared, always reaching beyond the distant horizon. European? Yes, but an ardent one, and that's what makes the difference between him and those for whom belonging to Europe comes cheap and almost feel forced to accept an EU passport. We consulted once with Dragan on a Lublin project for Western cultural managers and practitioners, which was meant to enable them to learn about Eastern Europe, entitled 'Abduction of Europe.' His reaction took us completely aback. He was not convinced by its mythological references, demanded that we change the title and warned us, like a father worrying about his child, against 'being led into temptation': irresponsible trifling with the project of uniting Europe, the most precious acquisition of our civilization for centuries. The same care told him to be at the same time critical and demanding, disciplined and pragmatic, the furthest possible from ideologies and mystifications as well as from the new European nationalism that instead of strengthening European identity in its openness and co-operation with other parts of the world locks it into a Europocentric backwater.

I met him for the first time twenty years ago, *Financial Times* in hand, and before our conversation moved towards Danilo Kiš[18] and Czesław Miłosz[19], I heard his analytical remarks concerning the economic situation of the world in which I heard a note of admiration for Balcerowicz's Plan[20]. We were united from the start by the borderland ethos and belonging to the Bosnian generation, one that saw the dramatic break-up of Yugoslavia, not a local Balkan conflict but a crisis of European culture. Along with it came a distancing from all European 'hypes' of the type of 'multi-culti' or 'intercultural dialogue' and criticism towards the 'festivalisation' of cultures, and the search for economy and rationality in cultural management, rather than indulging in uncritical financial claims. I had in Dragan a wonderful partner in my striving for an active, socially engaged culture, one valuing higher empathy over narcissism, and not giving up on inventiveness and high artistic ambitions. He hated kitsch as much as lack of punctuality, and he hated the lack of critical thinking the same way he hated verbosity. He was something of an

[18] Danilo Kiš (1935-1989), Serbian and Yugoslav novelist, short story writer and poet.
[19] Czesław Miłosz (1911-2004), Polish poet, prose writer and translator.
[20] The Balcerowicz Plan, method for rapidly transitioning from a communist economy, based on state ownership and central planning, to a capitalist market economy. Named after its author, the Polish minister and economist Leszek Balcerowicz, the plan was adopted in Poland in 1989.

aristocrat, the status he deserved not because of his inheritance but because of his acquired knowledge, sophisticated taste and penetrating intelligence. He used them not to 'serve at the court', but just the opposite - to mark his proud independence from authority, prejudice and coteries. And only in this sense I think about him as a real Prince of this unruly family of intellectuals, wandering artists, outsiders, exiles and rebels for whom Europe remains a still incompletely realised cultural project.

Dragan Klaic's legacy: Europe as a never ending conversation

Anne-Marie Autissier

Before I met Dragan, I edited some of his articles for *Culture Europe International*. At that time, we were a small team devoted to a quarterly magazine (in French and English) Culture Europe International that was trying to offer readers a comparative view of cultural policies and practices throughout Europe. I was actively looking for a specialist on Eastern and Central Europe. Odile Chenal (European Cultural Foundation) told me: "I know whom you need". That was in 1994. We started working together enthusiastically, and one day, finally, I met Dragan.

Since then, we never stopped writing to each other, exchanging ideas and projects. Dragan's universal curiosity was incredibly inspiring. However his main concern was about Europe: which Europe do we want? How can we strengthen the European will to create a shared vision? How to help Europe go beyond nationalisms? How to create a new European narrative thanks to the arts and culture? All those questions were common concerns.

One of my best memories of our work together is the *Culture Europe International* special issue which we set up in 2002, when he was chairing the European Forum for Arts and Heritage. At that time, the main concern – for the first time since World War Two – were the emerging right-wing populist political forces in the governments of Austria, the Netherlands, Italy, Denmark, Norway. That issue was dedicated to the cultural policies of the European right-wing populist political parties and movements. Dragan had thought of this particular thematic focus. Since then, I realised that few surveys had been carried out such as the one we did, with a comparative approach and an attempt to describe as well as possible, the cultural strategies adopted by those groups. This is a very promising field of research for the future – perhaps I should say 'unfortunately'.

Then in 2004 Dragan initiated EFRP, the European Festivals Research Project. From this viewpoint Dragan was courageous and he took risks. He wanted to gather researchers around the table, who were able to deepen the approaches applied to the study of festivals. The idea of setting up an interdisciplinary and multinational project dedicated to research what he called the 'Festival phenomenon' was challenging and pioneering.

ERFP was started as an informal research platform, which defined its research model and approach in Brussels in May 2004, this was built on at a researchers' meeting held at the *Divadelna Nitra Festival* in Slovakia in September 2005 and another one at De Montfort University in Leicester, England in March 2006, following a one-day conference for British festival practitioners and policy-makers, supported by the Arts Council England.

In May 2006 EFRP became a research consortium, consisting of the Budapest Observatory, De Montfort University, Fondazione Fitzcarraldo, Leiden University and Paris 8 University (Institute of European Studies), with the support of European Festivals Association and Arts Council England, and was joined in 2008 by Leeds Metropolitan University.

In Dragan Klaic's view, EFRP aimed to create a critical mass of research papers, studies, publications and debates in order to produce some tentative conclusions, trends and recommendations for festival practitioners and policy makers, public authorities, funders and existing and potential sponsors[21].

Looking at Europe today, I am tempted to write that Dragan left this world at the right time. But I do so in the knowledge that what Europe and Europeans are lacking today is the commitment of some personalities, some intellectuals with passion who are able to personify a new deal for Europe. More reports are not the answer as many have been completed and delivered, including many that are deeply critical of current economic, cultural and political policies of the European Union; but their impact has been limited. What Europe needs is people with the capacity to embody and deliver these important messages. Undoubtedly Dragan would have been one of those personalities and voices. This book reflects our will and commitment to carry on working towards a Europe united through culture.

---

[21] All articles and communications are available on the EFA website: http://www.efa-aef.eu.

Dragan Klaic
1950-2011
A reflection

Rose Fenton and Lucy Neal

It is with great sadness that we mark the passing of Dragan Klaic, a passionate European, a great intellectual force, an inspiring teacher, and a delightful, if at times maddening friend, who kept you on your toes with his quick thinking, provocative statements and challenging questions.

LIFT (London International Festival of Theatre) first encountered Dragan in 1993 the year after he had gone into voluntary exile following the bloody and traumatic breakup of Yugoslavia. In July 1993 the Bosnian capital of Sarajevo – Dragan's birthplace - was on the verge of collapse, as the Serbian forces closed in from the surrounding hills. That same week at the *LIFT Festival* a company made up of artists from across Bosnia, Serbia, Macedonia and Croatia were performing *Sarajevo*, a haunting lament for the ideals of a multi-cultural city that had been crushed as ethnic hatred inflamed its inhabitants. Dragan came over from Amsterdam, where he had just taken over as director of the Netherlands Theatre Institute, reconnecting with friends and colleagues from the former Yugoslavia and played a leading role in the debates we had organised with Amnesty International and The Refugee Council.

Over the subsequent years we would frequently run into Dragan at festivals and conferences; he would always be engaged in fierce debate, usually challenging the status quo – for which he often got into trouble - delivering diatribes against the pernicious effects of nationalism and parochialism; and promoting the imperative of the European cultural project.

Dragan was also passionate about festivals and was the initiator and chair of the European Festivals Research Project. So, in 2005, when we were writing *The Turning World, Stories from the London International Festival of Theatre*, it was very natural to ask Dragan to contribute an essay to our chapter on festivals. Writing in the *The Turning World* he coined the wonderfully evocative phrase describing festivals as experimental zones of sociability, going, in our view, to the heart of the festival spirit. In the same essay he also argued that "there was an urgent need for theatre to re-examine its social functions and reconsider its capacity to reshape the collective imagination and memory, to serve as a vehicle of debate, enhance intercultural relationships and affirm the public space as an essential feature of democracy." This is a subject he returned to in the book he had almost finished at the time of his death about the value of what he termed *public* as opposed to commercial theatre.

Lucy recalls:
Dragan has affected how I look and think about things. I am reminded of the 1970 picture of Joseph Beuys on the sofa, cradling an axe. This international work is not all comfy cushions. You need some metal in hand as well...! When engaging with Dragan, the combination of his humour, intellect and curiosity in what you had to say yourself made you sit up straight. No slouching.

The broad brush and close detail of a festival is a devilishly darned thing to describe to people, especially when your own ideas for its design are constantly on the move. The world's turning requires dexterous mapping: artistic experiments; socio-political shifts; paradigms to change and paradoxes to show. Dragan articulated our evolution of *LIFT* – sometimes better even than we could ourselves – with comic insight and charged sense of a utopia he believed festivals engendered. He knew in his bones they mattered and the vigilance with which their values of co-operation needed defending. The precision and humanity with which he spelt this out was and remains an inspiration. Carrying his ideals on is a shared challenge. No slouching Dragan!

Rose continues:

I was privileged to spend a great of time with Dragan in Lublin, Poland over the past two years. We were the so called 'international experts', along with the artist and writer Krzysztof Czyżewski, helping to develop the city's bid to become the European Capital of Culture 2016. On an almost monthly basis we would meet at 10pm at Warsaw airport, Dragan arriving either from his home in Amsterdam or from Budapest where he taught the MA Masters in Cultural Management at the Central European University. The car journey to Lublin would be filled with reflections on the state of Europe, gossip on the latest political scandal or bureaucratic incompetence, descriptions of the shows he'd seen on his travels – this opera in Budapest or Paris, that theatre show in Istanbul or Prague, and news of his family. Three hours later we would arrive at the Hotel Lublinianka where Dragan ensured a bottle of the best wine was waiting for us - and the conversation would continue far into the early hours. And then when I woke up in the morning at 8 a.m. there would always be several emails from Dragan in my in box! He was indefatigable.

Lublin loved Dragan. Even though true to form he ruffled a few feathers, not least when on our first visit he declared that the city could not possibly aspire to be European Capital of Culture if those working in the cultural sector did not speak English, the common language of communication across the continent. As a man who spoke nine languages fluently Dragan understood the power and value of language, and his instructions to the Mayor to set up compulsory English evening classes were carried out immediately.

Throughout the 90's as Europe came together once again following the collapse of communism, Dragan was an unstoppable force, developing programmes and projects to connect people – and particularly young people – across the continent. Over the past weeks since his death, I have met so many people, directors of festivals, theatres and cultural initiatives, particularly from Central and Eastern Europe, who said they would not be doing what they were doing without Dragan. He opened their minds, they said, gave them encouragement and courage. He was a wonderful - and a demanding - teacher.

In his book *The Mobility of the Imagination* Dragan lays out with 'Dragan- like' rigour and care the tools and philosophy of his 'intercultural –practice'.

Dragan we shall miss you hugely – your knowledge, your grasp of history, your ideals, your sense of fun, your combative yet generous spirit, and your warm and mischievous company.

The Future of
European Festivals

Bernard Faivre d'Arcier

Even if we sometimes trace the word 'festival' back to its ancient root (calling to mind the traditional events of Bayreuth, Orange and Verona), the idea of the arts festival as we know it is relatively recent. The modern festival has evolved as part of the 'leisure society', with its extended summer holidays and its all-pervasive media. The theatre festival in Avignon, the oldest and best known of all the French festivals, was founded in 1947 by actor and director Jean Vilar. Yet Vilar would never have imagined the success and geographical expansion that the future would bring to the festival phenomenon. For him, the festival was just another one of the many methods he used to bring young people together to share his aesthetic and moral values.

Immediately after the World War Two, festivals sprang up simultaneously in several countries. At the same time as Avignon and Aix-en-Provence were started in France, similar events in Edinburgh and Recklinghausen were born. This synchronicity implies that the festival is both a social and a historical phenomenon, one both rooted in and responding to the spirit of the times and to our consumer society.

Since then festivals have spread widely, to the extent that there are now innumerable iterations across the globe. Unfortunately it appears that we have now reached saturation point, and these events more often than not have become formulaic rather than more individual creative enterprises. Aren't there too many festivals now? Hasn't the public got tired of the very concept of a festival? Has the festival itself dissolved into just another facet of the tourism industry?

It is important to remember that festivals can play a significant role in introducing new works to the public. All over Western Europe more and more plays struggle to reach a wider audience, mainly in the world of public theatre, in countries where theatre comprises a multitude of small companies working on a project by project basis. While countries such as Germany or those in Central Europe perform repertory theatre so that actors are assured work all season, in France there is an imbalance between the number of plays produced and the availability of venues. This overproduction of plays can ultimately lead to media overkill and exhaust the interest of the public. Yet despite these problems, the festival is still capable of breathing fresh life into a city's theatrical scene: indeed, some plays are written with this exact revitalising purpose in mind. The festival can still serve to increase audience numbers and expand what Brecht called 'the circle of connoisseurs'.

While this all may be true of Western Europe, we cannot complain of the same level of saturation in the rest of the continent. Eastern Europe may have adopted the festival format some time ago, but there is still remarkably little opportunity to take shows from one country to another.

Does the festival still retain its original meaning? A festival is characterised by its exceptional nature. The word 'festival' is as synonymous with 'carnival' as it is 'estival' (a French term derived from the Latin word for 'summer', *aestivalis*). This exceptional nature is what has granted festivals such as Avignon or Edinburgh their longevity. (66 years, that is retirement age!) They offer a summer gathering over three or four weeks in a historic city, where all venues are accessible by foot, and where theatre lovers can unite in their shared passion.

Festivals have their fair share of detractors. Certain critics, often permanent institutions (such as the Centre Dramatique in France or the Teatro Stabile in Italy) frequently object to festivals as mere cultural frivolity. These institutions, because of their very permanence, take it upon themselves to act as cultural advisors and educators. Over time, this kind of objection has fortunately become less frequent for a number of reasons. Firstly there is the clear role which festivals play in initiating and teaching the public about theatre and other art forms, as well as their ability to lend a marked visibility to continuously operating venues and institutions. Secondly there is the fact that after a festival has taken place, arts groups know that they need only introduce festive moments to their annual programme to rekindle the flame of public interest.

So what is the point of festivals today?

Local politicians tend to justify official support for a festival in their city with reference to at least four reasons.

1) The first reason is the ability of the festival to democratise culture. A festival offers a far simpler introduction to the arts than those cultural institutions that we walk past every day and never enter (due for example to a lack of information, ticket prices, cultural barriers, fear of not being 'of that world'). At a festival, audiences are prepared to take risks. This is particularly the case in open air festivals, where people make the most of the summer and the holiday spirit by making friends, taking a chance on something together, flirting – and doing all this in a space where theatre is accessible, and where one can easily mingle with the performers.

These benefits also account for the success of street theatre and circus performers, without which many festivals would not be nearly so enjoyable. For many local politicians, the accessibility of the arts in the festival space is a useful tool to further the democratisation of culture.

2) Secondly, holding a festival serves as a means to forge new social connections and reinforce a sense of local identity. The festival can be a balm which heals social wounds; it can give rise to new friendships with neighbours or an intermingling of different groups, even if only for a moment. A festival can also give shape to a shared desire for identity, whether that is of a community, a neighbourhood, or of a professional environment.

3) The third argument, and surely the most recent and successful, is the idea that a festival provides a good economic opportunity. Over the last fifteen years, economic impact studies have convinced not only politicians but also shopkeepers and local businesses that a festival is, on the whole, a positive force in most economic sectors. The service industries are a good example: hotels, car parks, cafés, dry cleaners, souvenir shops and travel agents all can benefit from festivals.

4) Alongside the economic benefits, a festival brings visibility to any community which welcomes it - an image which it could not gain by other means. So the festival is often a key part of a local tourism policy which can extend well beyond the period of the festival itself. A city can also earn long-lasting prestige for only a fraction of what it would have to spend to achieve a similar result through advertising and media promotion. In fact, a good festival can create much more media coverage than any publicity campaign for considerably less expenditure.

5) Obviously, there is a fifth and final reason for the existence of festivals, and in fact it is the most important (although it does not always receive a mention when it should): festivals have unique artistic and cultural value.

- Artistic in the sense that if a festival has the desire and means to truly engender creativity, it will encourage its artists to dare to change their habits and locales, permitting them to reinvent themselves and to break free from conventional modes of performance and artistic production. During a festival, a play can last half an hour or an entire night. It could be played out in Korean or Turkish, or even in an incredible space where a play would never normally be performed. A festival must always create a space for risks to be taken.

- The cultural value of festivals lies in the fact that they present an opportunity for audiences to discover new things (for just like the artist, the audience itself takes more risks), a chance to learn and to discuss with like-minded people. Festivals are great occasions for debate, whether formal or informal: at a festival, words, rumours and reputations run wild. Most festivals are places where different aesthetics and disciplines meet and confront each other on an international scale. They also provide a unique opportunity for artists to meet their public, and for the critic him/herself to be criticised.

Two distinct types of festival have evolved in recent years:

1) Some festivals – particularly those in big capitals – have transformed themselves into 'seasons' by lengthening their duration and making space for multiple artistic disciplines. These festivals programme works from a diverse range of foreign countries in order to encourage international artistic exchange, some alternatively choosing a particular theme or contributors from a specific region. This can lead to a festival becoming somewhat diluted. These festivals may lack the Aristotelian unities of place, time and action. If they do not take place in a centralised space, the public may feel

that they are not living the festival experience. What is more plays, for example, are generally performed in different spaces; one night in the town centre, another in the suburbs. In these circumstances the festival, which is often not allocated its dedicated space, must come to an agreement with existing theatres and superimpose its own image onto that of its host. We can see examples of this in Paris (*Festival d'Automne*), Tokyo, Berlin, and Rome (*Romaeuropa*).

This sense of dilution is accentuated by the lengthening of the festival's run, which makes it lose the unique quality of a concentrated event, and perhaps even surrender the explosive impact of performance. In such cases, the festival plays more on the reputation of its brand. These festivals need to be known as not-to-miss events to win the loyalty of the public. The unfortunate result of this is that it distances the artists from their audiences, making the exciting communication between the two more difficult and uncertain. In this way festivals which run for too long court the risk of losing their exceptional character. However they may also be said to enrich the theatrical, musical and choreographic life of their cities thanks to their selection of works and their international reputation.

2) The other possible evolution of the festival format is quite the opposite: they are cut extremely short and can be reduced to only a weekend or even a single night, which can result in large attendance figures and increased media coverage. We can see this evolution in the *Nuits Blanche*[22] which take place in Paris one night in October, a format which has already been adopted by scores of cities throughout the world. At the moment this format is mainly centred on the visual arts, although theatre, music and other cultural forms are often also incorporated. These festivals rely on huge crowds which, while they may not be able to see everything, may still discover or rediscover monuments and open spaces in an unusual or original way. These kinds of events are a godsend for the fickle media which rarely covers longer artistic events for their whole duration. On the other hand, these one-night festivals make it impossible for people to see everything, and so their experience of the arts may become somewhat

[22] Launched by the Mayor of Paris in October 2002, and every year since, the 'Nuit Blanche' (white night in French) is an annual all-night or night-time arts festival. Based on an idea first developed in Helsinki and Nantes, a 'Nuit Blanche' will typically have museums, private and public art galleries, and other cultural institutions open and free of charge, with the centre of the city itself being turned into a de facto art gallery, providing space for art installations, performances (music, film, dance, performance art), themed social gatherings, and other activities.

impoverished. They operate in the spirit of our age of advertising and hedonism, providing a short-lived pleasure.

The fact remains that arts festivals retain their legitimacy as long as they endeavour to support artistic creativity, particularly at an international level. The true role of a festival is to encourage artists to dare and to undertake projects that they might not risk while working in more permanent institutions.

List of European Festival Research Programme Workshops

Brussels, May 2004: an informal research gathering at which participants discussed and defined an approach to research for EFRP.

Nitra, September 2005, hosted by *Divadelna Nitra Festival*. Focus: festivals and their impacts.

Leicester, March 2006, hosted by De Montfort University. Focus: the local impact of arts festivals with an international agenda. This workshop followed a one-day international conference, 'Challenges of Growth', aimed at the British arts festivals sector and supported by Arts Council England.

Le Mans, November 2006, hosted by FranceFestivals. Focus: the sustainability of festivals.

Barcelona, October 2007, hosted by InterArts and presented in conjunction with the CIRCLE network of cultural policy researchers. Focus: a roundtable discussion on the festival policies of public authorities, one outcome of which was a set of policy recommendations.

Helsinki, April 2008, hosted by the City of Helsinki Culture Department. Focus: the urban impact of artistic festivals.

Moscow, October 2008, hosted by *Big Break*, Moscow International Festival of Theatre for Children. Focus: theatre festivals for children.

Novi Sad, May 2009, hosted and organised by the *Sterijino pozorje*, a festival of performances in association with the International Association of Theatre Critics. Focus: international theatre festivals and audience development.

Leeds, November 2009, hosted by the UK Centre for Events Management and the Cultural Policy and Planning Unit, Leeds Metropolitan University. Focus: the governance and leadership of arts festivals.

Poznań, April 2010, hosted by the Institute of Cultural Studies, Adam Mickiewicz University, Poznań. Focus: artistic festivals with a social and intellectual agenda.

Strasbourg, April 2011, hosted by Groupe de Sociologie Politique Européenne, University of Strasbourg. Focus: festivals, municipalities and metropolises.

Maribor, October 2011, hosted by Festival *Borštnikovo Srečanje*. Focus: artistic festivals and continuously operating cultural organisations.

Index of Names

Notes on Contributors

Autissier, Anne-Marie

Anne-Marie Autissier is Director of the Institute of European Studies at Paris 8 University. Her main research interests include: a comparative study of cultural policies in Europe; the role of art festivals in transnational cooperation; cultural radio channels in France and Europe.

Bianchini, Franco

Franco Bianchini is Professor of Cultural Policy and Planning at Leeds Metropolitan University. From 1992-2007 he was Reader in Cultural Planning and Policy and Course Leader for the MA in European Cultural Planning at De Montfort University, Leicester.

Czyżewski, Krzysztof

Krzystof Czyżewski is a co-founder and president of the Borderland Foundation (1990) and director of the Borderland of Arts, Cultures and Nations Centre in Sejny. In 2011 he opened the International Centre for Dialog in Krasnogruda on the Polish-Lithuanian border.

Faivre d'Arcier, Bernard

Bernard Faivre d'Arcier served for a first time as director of the *Avignon Festival* in 1980-84. He was then appointed as cultural advisor to the Prime Minister and in 1986 he launched the television channel La Sept, the French arm of the Franco-German channel Arte. From 1993 to 2003, Faivre d'Arcier was appointed for a second time as the director of Avignon Festival. He is presently consultant for many culture institutions, and chairs la *Biennale de Lyon*.

Fenton, Rose

Rose Fenton is the Director of Free Word (London, UK). Between 1980 and 2005 Rose was cofounder and codirector of the London International Festival of Theatre (LIFT).

Maughan, Christopher

Christopher Maughan is Associate Research Fellow in Arts and Festivals Management at De Montfort University. His work on festivals led to his University being a founder member of the European Festival Research Project.

Neal, Lucy

Lucy Neal is the Former Co-Director and Co-founder of London International Festival of Theatre (LIFT).

The Budapest Observatory

The Budapest Observatory was created in 1999. Its mission is to be of help for those, who want to know more about the ways cultural life is being financed in Europe, more particularly in East-Central European countries. As a resource organisation, the Budapest Observatory facilitates research, collects and provides information, establishes contacts in areas.